Bodylessons

Exploring the Wisdom of Your Body

by

Marian Wolfe Dixon

FINDHORN
Press

First published by Findhorn Press 2005

ISBN 1-84409-062-0

British Library Cataloguing-in-Publication Data.
A catalogue record for this book is available
from the British Library.

Edited by Shari Mueller
Cover design by Damian Keenan
Interior design by Asiatype, Inc.

Printed and bound in the USA

Published by
Findhorn Press
305A The Park,
Findhorn, Forres
Scotland IV36 3TE
Tel 01309 690582
Fax 01309 690036
email: info@findhornpress.com
www.findhornpress.com

Contents

Introduction

The mystery of the soul is revealed in the
movement of the body.
– Michelangelo Buonarrot

This book is about a new kind of learning – or rather an old kind of knowing – the knowing of the body. It is the knowing of ourselves as physical beings. It is the knowing that we derive from movement.

Humans are physical entities. From conception until death, we live in physical bodies. This does not mean that we are the **same** as our physical shells. What it does mean is that we wear our bodies like a suit of clothes and that these clothes shape the way we move, act, feel and think. The body is the physical counterpart of our entire life history. All the problems and pleasures of the inner life coexist with the life of the body. The body is the instrument for many of our most intimate relationships and experiences. Encounters with exultation and pain are clothed in physical sensations. Building a dialog with the body can establish access to its natural wisdom and provide a way to apply that wisdom to every aspect of our lives.

Human life means movement. From the day we are born to the day we die, our bodies move, in one way or another, to keep us alive. Movement transmits sensory information about where body parts are and how they feel. When you are hurt, ill, or stop moving for other reasons, the neural circuits that transmit sensory and motor information become less effective. Muscles work best when exercised and allowed to move freely. Inaction is an unnatural state for living animals. Even when we are asleep the heart pumps, the blood circulates, the chest rises and falls, and a myriad of other activities integral to human survival takes place.

Kinesthetic Knowing

The ancient Greeks recognized that studying movement could help them with imponderables such as "What is the world made of?" and "Why is it the way it is?" Greek students were exposed to mathematics, literature, music, poetry, writing, **and** gymnastics (physical education). Every citizen was encouraged to fully develop kinesthetic talents. Physical education was an important avenue for coping with and understanding their physical world.

Even today, the importance of kinesthetic knowing is recognized. According to Howard Gardner's *Frames of Mind: The Theory of Multiple Intelligences,* each child is born with not one but seven distinct types of intelligence. These seven ways of knowing are linguistic (language), logical-mathematical (symbols), visual-spatial (images), bodily-kinesthetic (physical), musical (sounds), interpersonal (social), and intrapersonal (spiritual). Every individual is said to partake of all seven types of intelligence. But not everyone partakes of them to the same degree. Each person has a personal learning style emphasizing certain ways of knowing over others.

Verbal and mathematical/logical abilities are the two types of intelligence that show up on standardized tests. In our society, we have no authenticated way of measuring other forms of intelligence. Since we cannot measure other types of knowing, our society affords them less recognition and respect. Children who are good with words and logic are rewarded with praise and good grades. Children who show promise in dance, art, music, social relations, intuition, or drama tend not to receive the same recognition. There is even less material appreciation for adults with skills in areas that are not firmly based in the verbal or rational. This imbalance may be one reason that well-known entertainers get paid so highly. We value most what we lack in ourselves. Through passive observation of our favorite entertainers, we are desperately trying to regain parts of ourselves that have not been allowed to blossom and grow.

A more supportive environment would be sensitive to individual variations in the way we learn, and would nurture and facilitate many different types of learning. Many of us never tap into most of our intelligences, and this may be the reason why some students fail to learn in traditional schools. We must begin to value all of the ways in which we know.

Not only do we neglect physical knowledge, but also when we recognize a neglected ability, we tend to categorize and isolate it from other ways of knowing. For example, in our society athletes are not considered to be introspective. Artists are categorized as airheads, incapable of logic. Intellectuals are said to lack street smarts. All of us, athletes and intellectuals alike, would be better off, if we engaged in more activities that allowed us to use and develop our intelligences in tandem.

The goal of this book is to illuminate the many lessons that the physical body has to share. Hopefully, *Bodylessons* can help integrate neglected body wisdom with more conventional understanding about ourselves and the world in which we live. Life of the body parallels the movement of inner life. The life history of our psyche and soma act as mirrors for one another, although each retains its own perspective and style – physical and psychological share in the experience of the whole human being. The successes or frustrations of one are reflected in the strengths or weaknesses of the other. I believe that building an understanding of ourselves as physical organisms helps reinforce all our intelligences. Incorporating body wisdom into our worldview makes us smarter and more vital beings.

Note: Each of the seven types of knowing is activated in the experience of a Bodylesson.

- Concepts in *Bodylessons* are based on connections found in language. Meanings of terms and word relationships between physical attributes and corresponding mental and emotional traits are highlighted.
- Symbolic/logical learning is fostered when readers are challenged to think through the theory behind *Bodylessons*. Those who explore the Body Work exercises at the end of each chapter must logically deduce how bodies can solve a particular challenge.
- Insofar as physical bodies move through and are situated in space, *Bodylessons* promotes spatial knowing. Specific exercises are provided in the chapter on **time** and **space**.
- Practicing the Body Work and other exercises promotes body/kinesthetic development. Physical learning IS the point of *Bodylessons*.

- Through this book, motion becomes a way of celebrating sound and movement heightens the experience of changing rhythms and tunes. See the chapter on **time** for specific exercises.
- The chapter on **relationships** and **reaction** is particularly attuned to social learning.
- All lessons depend on inner sensations, thoughts and feelings. Intrapersonal experiences are fostered throughout and are paramount in the chapters on **awareness** and **focus**.

Participation versus Performance

Movement is usually practiced with an eye towards a future goal. Weekend athletes work on their golf swing with the tournament in mind, and dancers rehearse pirouettes in preparation for a spotlighted role. We encourage our children to practice softball so that their team will win the big game, or ballet so that their performance in the semi-annual dance concert will make us proud.

Consider instead the notion that movement is valuable not only as a means to an end, i.e., performance, but that moving our body has value, in and of itself. The real value of movement comes with participation in its flow. "Sure," I can hear you say, "movement is worthwhile. Otherwise we would always be still. How could I argue with that?" But if you nod in assent complacently, consider whether your actions reaffirm your words, or not. Do you experience most movement as a repetitive, even boring, price to pay to reach a sought after goal? Do you exercise your body only for future payoffs like a slimmer body, thicker biceps, or a tougher tennis swing? How often do you participate in movement for the sheer joy that it brings? Do you experience the joy of motion as a spectator only? (e.g., "How about those Redskins?" or "My boy, Tom, made a fantastic catch in left field!")

All of us are natural athletes but something happens to make us forget that. We become self-conscious, embarrassed about our bodies, and convinced that our actions are awkward and ugly. Unless we move with the grace of Ginger Rogers or the confidence of Michael Jordan, we are afraid to move. We find ourselves sitting back and becoming spectators. Making excuses, we begin to see movement as something frivolous and unimportant.

This sad state of affairs need not be the case for anyone. I personally have danced with three- and four-year-olds, people over eighty-five, patients recovering from strokes and other degenerative diseases and people who were visually impaired or blind. From these experiences, I know that everyone can move and everyone can dance – they do not need to talk or see, they don't even need to walk. I have seen patients in wheelchairs share the joy that comes with movement. Experience has convinced me that everyone can dance, and more importantly, that everyone needs to. Moving our bodies is a source of wonder and joy. Wonder and joy are not frivolous; they are precious and profound qualities of life. Creative movement can cheer our souls and make even the sad times worth living. Physical activity, like life, is most meaningful when we participate. It is not enough to simply perform; neither is it sufficient to sit back and watch someone else.

Writing this book is a way of sharing some of the joy that movement has brought to my life. Physical activity has helped me at times when I could not talk about my feelings. Dancing has been a comfort when other sources of light seemed to dim. When I was feeling confused and not trusting my thoughts or emotions, my body was an anchor. I trust my body. It tells me its truth. It tells me when I am stiff and need to move, or when I am hungry and need to be filled. The body can be such a source of light and inspiration, if only we remember to listen to its wisdom. The process of moving is a teacher about so many things in life – how to express myself, what are my attitudes, how to make use of time, how to move through space, and how to encounter the force and the weight of other physical entities. In short, my own body literally contains answers to questions about how to experience everything that I do.

Initiation versus Imitation

Most movement classes require students to imitate exercises rather than initiate creative solutions to kinesthetic problems. The instructor points her toe . . . you point your toe. The instructor raises her left arm . . . you follow suit. The instructor demonstrates or explains in detail a complex sequence of steps and students are expected to learn the steps by imitating them. So you do your best to comply.

Indeed, there is much inherent value in the imitative act. As children, we learn how to function in society by modeling the actions of others. We learn to talk, walk, spell, read, add numbers, and master various other necessities of life by copying what others teach us. All our lives we continue to learn by adopting the admired (and sometimes not so admired) traits of those around us. When special role models do not take us by the hand, sometimes we turn to professionals for help. These helpers show us new ways that imitation can be a means for growth. Modeling is used by psychotherapists and other members of the 'helping professions' to show clients how to deal with situations that they cannot master on their own.

And imitating can be fun. The game of 'monkey see – monkey do', although an irritation to the ones who are mocked, is pleasurable to the one who imitates everything they see and hear others do.

With so many advantages to learning by imitation, why would anyone want to teach movement any other way? What can one gain from learning by initiation, interpretation and facilitation that they cannot get from modeling?

As a partial answer to this question, let us look to the teachings of two philosophers. These 'lovers of learning', Plato and Ram Dass, hail from very different eras but have similar messages about the value of initiative learning.

Plato, the classical Greek scholar and some say mystic, introduced the character of Socrates and his method for teaching. The Socratic method involves continual questioning by the teacher of his students. The teacher/tutor does not provide information 'on a plate', but instead acts like a midwife to draw truth out from the student. The search for inner knowledge and individual understanding is an integral part of the Socratic method.

Ram Dass, a modern-day truth seeker, relates a story about the difference between the two kinds of learning. In one story, God and Satan were walking together along the street when the Lord bent down and picked something up. Satan asked God, "What is it that you have there?"

The Lord gazed at the thing, glowing brightly in his hand, and replied, "This is Truth." Satan reached out for it saying, "Here, let me have it. I'll organize it for you."

Both the Socratic method and Ram Dass' story indicate that we can learn to know and think as individuals. We can design our lives and actions from an inner psyche rather than from rules, idols, or status symbols of the outer world. *Bodylessons* provides a way to track daily life from the vantage point of your own body and its unique qualities and capabilities. Learning to trust this knowledge and becoming familiar and comfortable with our bodies can show how we need not always look to others for help or reassurance. When solving a problem of how to move in the most relaxed or efficient way, at a certain point it is necessary to let go of all outside help and focus in on our own strength and resourcefulness. When we mechanically adjust ourselves to rules prescribed by some outside expert, we exchange a fuller experience of life for something less. On the other hand, using motion and body awareness to creatively understand our lives can be a wonderful alternative.

Resistance to Learning by Initiation

There is often resistance against a learning process that promulgates self-searching and discovery. In our society, there is resistance to methods that do not teach inviolable and unquestioned 'truths'. Public education in America has traditionally relied heavily on simple regurgitation of memorized information. Unfortunately, as we age, much of the memorized information is forgotten.

As a teacher/trainer for many years, I have observed great resistance to creative learning. Most surprising was the source of this resistance. The greatest protests against creative problem solving did not stem from fellow instructors, nor from parents, administrators or counselors, but from students themselves. Many students in my college classes have rarely, if ever, been encouraged to create something new. They rebel against having to do anything that they have not been shown exactly how to do. They are uncomfortable learning when their answers cannot be checked against a correct response. But once students get past their initial discomfort, it is amazing how quickly they open to the discovery process and how eager they are to meet new challenges head (and toes) on.

What Kind of Lessons

What wonderful lessons there are to learn! The body never lies. It tells us when we are ill, nervous, or in pain. The body knows everything. And it can share that knowledge if we will only listen to its cues.

A human body functions by principles that are universal to the species, and each individual body is unique. Each body builds its own life history with its own unique combination of activities and experiences. Every physical body has been shaped by a past, lives in a present, and moves toward a future. But the events and influences of the past, present, and future are unique for each individual. Thus, to obtain any real knowledge about the body, one must examine one's own physical self.

Each Chapter Equals a Lesson

This text treats physical characteristics as topics for self-investigation. Some topics (e.g., **posture** or **attitude, focus,** and **flexibility**) lead us to discover more about physical bodies without regard to an outside world. Other traits (e.g., **time** and **space, weight, relationships,** and **reaction** vs. **response**) help define our bodies in an external physical reality. Each chapter is devoted to one of these *Bodylessons*, so named because each lesson is one that the body shares with the whole self. The body can experience a lesson about **focusing,** for example, that will better enable the whole self to focus when life requires it. Each chapter in the manuscript provides both a conceptual framework and experiential exercises (called Body Work) for the selected Bodylesson. The conceptual discussions are designed to stimulate the reader to think about the intricate network of relationships between body, mind, and emotions. Solving the Body Work problems/exercises at the end of each chapter will help the active reader to incorporate the psychological/physical connections in a kinesthetic way.

The Bodylessons are not a new discipline or physical regimen that must be followed with rigid accuracy in order to achieve results. It would be much more helpful to think of the lessons as options or jumping-off points for exploration. The best expert for what you can learn from a Bodylesson is **you**. If a technique that is described in this book works for you, that is wonderful! By all means use it. But if a concept or an exercise is not helpful, let it go. Not all techniques work for everyone.

Although Bodylessons is not a discipline in itself, the lessons do draw on the age-old wisdom of many established practices. Long before modern times, people realized that certain types of physical training had dramatic and beneficial effects not only for the body, but also for the whole self. In this book, I share the lessons I have gleaned from the practice and study of such diverse disciplines as hatha yoga, dance and improvisation, tai chi, psychocalisthenics, aikido, massage, and other relaxation and coping techniques. These disciplines are profiled in the final chapter of the book.

The Conceptual Framework

Bodylessons relies heavily on the premise that wisdom of the body can translate into wisdom of the psyche. What evidence exists to convince us that the body can be connected with the mind and emotions? How do we know that such a connection could be useful? Although relationship between mind, body, emotions, and spirit has not yet been completely charted, there is a well-known paradigm for inter-relationships of the mind, body and emotions as they relate to the stress response. In essence, the model includes a stimulus, mental response, emotional response, physical response, and finally disease resulting from stress.

An environmental stimulus is the first event to trigger the stress reaction. The event can be anything from a loud noise to a reprimand from the boss. Any demand – physical or mental – can act as a stimulus. At this step in the process you analyze and categorize the environmental stimulus. It is here that labels, such as 'good' or 'bad', 'threatening' or 'harmless', are attached to the event. If a stimulus is perceived as a stressor, emotional arousal is evoked. Arousal can be from positive emotions such as joy, excitement, or ecstasy as well as negative emotions such as sadness, fear or anger.

Physical response occurs via a dual control made up of the nervous and endocrine systems. The nervous system uses electrical impulses from the brain and spinal cord to directly innervate selected organs in the body. The endocrine system utilizes chemical messengers called hormones that travel through the circulatory system. The electrical and/or chemical messages spark measurable changes in the functioning of targeted organs. Some common effects include elevated heart rate and blood pressure, perspiration, dilation of the pupils of the eyes, dilation of air passageways in the lungs, increased oxygen consumption, increased muscle tension, and decreased gastro-intestinal activity. If the physical changes (e.g., elevated pulse and blood pressure) are sustained over an extended period, disease will result.

The following example may help to personalize the stress model and make it more relevant to our own experience. Joanne left for work late this morning. She was trying to make up some of the time by driving 45 miles per hour in a 35 mile per hour zone. Joanne is speeding along without a care in the world when she hears a siren and spots a spinning light on top of the car behind. She pulls over to the side of the road and stops, and a policewoman walks up to the window. As Joanne accepts the citation, she also receives the environmental stimulus we mentioned earlier. When Joanne thinks to herself, "Boy, am I a jerk! That's my third ticket this year," her mental perception and appraisal are kicking in. Emotional arousal (fear and self-reproach) follow this thought and the illogical thought that, "Jeez, my husband's going to want a divorce!" Finally, Joanne's sweaty palms, fast-beating heart, and quick, shallow breathing are clear demonstrations of the physical arousal that she experiences as a result of the stressful event.

Now if Joanne's body, mind, and emotions consistently react to stressors in this way, sooner or later she will become ill. But if Joanne can manage to interrupt the chain of events at any point, she can prevent psycho-somatic disease and make a significant change in the quality of her life. Let us see how some 'interruptions' of the cycle could have been achieved.

The environmental stimulus could have been eliminated if Joanne had chosen to drive slower and risk being late, or if she had gotten up earlier and planned enough time to allow a leisurely trip. A new mental percep-tion and appraisal could be something like, "Even though I got a ticket this morning, I am still a capable and worthwhile person. My husband will still love me. Getting a ticket is no grounds for divorce." Emotional arousal is often the hardest link in the stress chain to extinguish. In the heat of the moment, emotions can erupt so quickly and forcefully that they are hard to stop. But you can prepare in advance for the kinds of emotions that habitually appear. Or you can deal with feelings after a situation has blown over, by talking them out with a counselor or a trusted friend, or by reporting them in a journal. The last link in the chain, physical arousal, is one of the easiest to break. The body's response to stress can be modified with easily learned relaxation skills such as diaphragmatic breathing, progressive muscular relaxation or visualiza-tion. (These techniques are described in subsequent chapters of *Bodylessons*.)

Conceptualizing a relationship between body, mind, and emotions helps us to see how stress, a maladaptive physical response, may be managed. Conversely, we may be able to consciously encourage healthier mental and emotional responses by changing the way we move the body. The Bodylessons are lessons about the body, but they are also lessons for the whole self.

The Physical/Kinesthetic Exercises (Body Work)

A conceptual approach, by itself, is not enough. Mind-body relationships must be experienced in order to be truly understood. When one asks the question, "What does it mean to be alive?" it is likely that first the intel-lect will grope for concepts, theories, or words to explain. The mental center, however, can only think about life. Mind alone is unable to absorb life in all its immediacy, in the here and now.

Young animals and children seem to be aware of their lives in a more direct, uncomplicated way. Young creatures respond with their whole selves, not just with their heads. Sometimes with the aid of nature even an adult can get a sense of immediate contact with life. Deep in the woods, on the top of a mountain, watching the waves of the ocean or the babbling of a stream, we feel life pulsing through everything, taking on different shapes and forms and yet, itself, changeless. Some call this experience 'being at one with nature'; others call it 'being aware of God'. In any case, it is our experience, not some abstract notion, that teaches us the deepest truths about being alive.

Combining Concepts with Experience Equals Understanding

Although all creatures can experience life's kinesthetic truths, only an adult human being (as far as we know) can have a deep experience and know that (s)he is having it. The Bodylessons ask readers to pause and reflect upon the experience of life in a new way. The lessons show how the most important thing about life is that we are alive, here and now, in a universe where everything around us is alive also. Not to experience life in all its manifold expressions is to be dead. *Bodylessons* asks you to consider, to sense, and to feel what it is like to live in a physical body. When you do, you cannot help but wonder at the wisdom that the human body holds.

*   *   *   *   *

Before we can even begin to reflect upon mental, emotional, or kinesthetic experiences, we must first confront the experiences as they really are. We need to base our investigations not on what we imagine or desire, but on what we see. A basic and fundamental tool that is used in all of the subsequent Bodylessons is **awareness**. Awareness helps us to take in life-experiences as a whole, without judging or denying certain parts as unworthy, unimportant, or just plain bad. In the first chapter, we examine this most fundamental process of Awareness.

Chapter 1

AWARENESS
The Key to Linking Concepts and Experience

This, too, can be experienced with a completely
expanded awareness.
– Thaddeus Golas

Sometimes I think the attitude of most people towards awareness is indifferent at best. "Why are you telling me to be aware? What do you think I am doing? I **am** aware! How could I be awake and responding to influences in the world if I were not aware?" And to a certain degree, this is true.

Associated Concepts

It is no coincidence that the admonition, 'beware', is a contraction of the words 'be aware'. Certainly, one of the things that we need to be aware of is danger. Unfortunately the contraction also reflects a deep-seated fear on our part of being aware. We feel that we must 'beware' of what we are really thinking, feeling, sensing, acting, and doing. Gurdjieff suggests that this is because we do not wish to disturb the comfort and ease of habitual patterns. We do not wish to 'wake up' to those things that make our life real, because we fear that we may see some terrible things. "If I were more aware of all the things that are wrong in my life and in the lives of others, I would really go crazy!"

Peak Experiences

I would bet that we have all experienced special moments when the senses are more keenly tuned, when the motor responses are at their peak, when we are functioning at our very best. Athletes report experiencing this kind of heightened awareness in the midst of 'peak performances'. For a gymnast, it may be a recognition that a tiny part of the routine flows. Even before seeing the scores, she knows that she just completed the most perfect back flip of her life.

As a person who loves to dance, I have experienced the feeling of being truly aware as a part of dance. I have also experienced peak awarenesses in my role as a teacher. Sometimes a realization occurs for me during a lecture or discussion. When my students and I are working together at a smooth, attuned level, I am somehow able to sense exactly what the class needs to hear and am able to respond accordingly. Words (and/or actions) seem to flow in just the right way. Many times what students ask is not really what they want to know. Something in me can sense what my pupils are really reaching for and how to touch them on that expanded level.

Nature

Performance is neither a necessary component nor a key ingredient of awareness. Often individuals report an expanded perception that accompanies communing with nature. Some remember a special time in a meadow. For others, the magical place may be beside a stream, overlooking the Grand Canyon, or close to the ocean's thundering surf. The majesty of a beautiful setting seems to spark a 'mind-fullness' in many human beings.

Then again, there are accounts of clear awareness when no grand aspect is involved, whatsoever. Mindfulness can occur during a peaceful moment at home, drinking a cup of tea, washing the dishes, or even sitting alone, quiet and still.

The 'Eidos'

Plato identifies several levels of awareness in *The Republic* where he introduces the 'Divided Line' as a conceptual device. Let us see how something, like a sphere, might be perceived differently depending on the level of awareness brought to the task. At one level is the shadowy image of a sphere. Perhaps we see a reflection of a ball in water or as a shadow on the ground. The form is quite distorted; it may be rippling or lengthened. At another level is a physical ball. It is round, solid, maybe hard, maybe soft. At a third level we might perceive the orderly relationships and processes inherent in each sphere (e.g., [pi = 3.14 . . .] multiplied by the diameter of the sphere always describes the circumference of that sphere). At the top level is **the sphereness** of the sphere, what Plato calls the 'eidos', and which we roughly translate as 'the idea'. This is a kind of blueprint for the sphere, which all spheres share, and which I dare to call the 'spirit' of the thing.

Awareness of Movement

Observing ourselves as we move allows us to more fully experience our physicality. We see less of the distortion and more of our true essence. We gain a new and expanded awareness of ourselves as physical entities. This tells us more about ourselves, for after all, we are material beings. Just as greater mindfulness can lead us to the 'eidos' or 'spirit' of the sphere, so might mindfulness of our physical selves lead us back to an experience of our bodies as an expression of spirit.

The notion of using expanded self-awareness to achieve a better life is also not new. Since the advent of Sigmund Freud and his tool of psychoanalysis, a host of psychological therapies have advocated detailed analyses of the self with the purpose of making the self more well and whole. Molly Groger applies the skills of *Eating Awareness Training* to help people achieve optimum weight levels without dieting. Richard Carson speaks of 'taming the gremlin' within us all through techniques of staying in the present moment and not judging. In the 1950's, Carl Rogers began advocating the use of simple awareness techniques as counseling tools in his highly regarded client-centered therapy. And centuries before modern times, Zen and buddhism promulgated non-judgment and staying in the moment.

What is new here is how the self-awareness is applied. The Bodylessons and Body Work exercises in this chapter apply a variety of contemplative techniques (e.g., not judging and centering in the here and now) to the task of observing how living bodies move, work, and play. Why? Because focusing on physicality is a useful tool for grounding thoughts and emotions in reality. Also, it feels good to allow more freedom into the body. *Bodylessons* is intended not only as a source of knowledge, but also as a source of joy.

Observing

Do you remember as an infant, the experience of catching sight of one of your own hands and being filled with a sense of wonder? Unfortunately, for most of us, this power of wonder about our own bodies is left back in childhood. As adults, we tend to take our bodies for granted in a dull kind of way and only attend to them after we discover pain, injury, or 'dis-ease'. We unconsciously relegate the life of the body to a position of being indistinguishable from any other kind of life possible for us. Although we can be driven to all sorts of extremes by the needs, desires, wants, and appetites of the physical body, and although we alternately abuse or indulge the body's whims, we rarely stop to perceive what a healthy body is. We rarely entertain the idea that we can contribute substantially to own health and well-being.

So it would be wise to save some awareness for the physical aspect of life. It would be useful to ask ourselves, "What can my body do?" "What does it like to do?" "What are my physical possibilities?" "What are my body's limitations?" "How does my body function?" and "How do I experience physicality in a meaningful way?"

Experiencing

In order to establish the function of a machine it is necessary to really look at it. If I look at my physical body as an instrument, and if I can see the instrument more clearly, I may better discern its purposes. What knowledge and understanding could be more vital than the understanding of myself as a corporeal being? One can scarcely study the human body even a little without becoming aware that it is indeed a finely-tuned instrument, a working, functioning unit. It never fails to amaze me how a human body has the capacity to take care of itself. The body can, for the most part, maintain itself in a healthy and operational state. When we sustain a small cut or bruise, physical bodies demonstrate a miraculous capacity to heal. Most wondrous of all, human beings can reproduce and create new life. Completely new people, entities that are both alike and unlike both parents, are born. The miracle of birth is appreciated more as an experience than an intellectual endeavor.

One can intellectually learn from anatomy and physiology source books, that the brain regulates bodily functions. According to such scientific texts, the brain takes care of the digestion of food, circulation of blood, inhalations and exhalations, and elimination of wastes. None of this do I voluntarily **do** for myself. None of this do I observe, except in the most superficial way. (Except for times when I voluntarily take over the regulation of my breathing. However, for most of my waking hours and when I am asleep and not conscious, my body still breathes and I continue to live.) In my day-to-day existence, I ordinarily do not take the time to observe the way that I am breathing, nor do I observe the feeling of blood as it courses throughout my body, nor do I look for any of the other crucial physiological functions that keep me alive.

In order to truly understand the apparatus of the physical body, knowledge that we glean from kinesiology, anatomy, physiology and other third-person-based scientific texts must be supplemented with first-hand experience. Some of our most useful information comes through continual self study and report. Second-hand knowledge about the way bodies are supposed to function (whether derived from books, lectures, slide shows, or even from the almighty statistical research study) cannot take the place of knowing that comes from listening to what a body has to say.

Observe. Human bodies are alive. They move and they function. The body has its own intelligence. Use *Bodylessons* to better understand and assimilate knowledge that your body wants to share. Be curious and ask many, many questions. Ask, "How do I move?" "How do I bend?" "How do I turn?" "How is the way that I move different from the way that my friend moves?" and "How do we both perform our functions in a wonderfully divine, unique, and special way?" Most importantly, enjoy learning about yourself with *Bodylessons*.

Awareness Applied to Relationships

Although the emphasis here is on expanding awareness of your physical body, heightened awareness can affect other aspects of life as well. Mindfulness of the body can signal mental and emotional effects that other people have on you. Attending to your own body language, for example, can be a cue to thoughts and feelings that you may be hiding, even from yourself. The next time you find yourself leaning forward, pay attention. Are you expending needless energy or intruding on other people's space? When you find yourself leaning way back, it may be that others are coming at you too strongly. Contrast the times when you lean with times when you are standing or sitting erect with relaxed shoulders. Usually an erect posture puts you in a position of balance and centeredness and signals to others that you are very much in control.

You can also become more aware of the effect others have on you by looking at your thoughts. What do you think about when you are near certain people? With one friend, you may find yourself drawn toward happy thoughts. With another, you may always be contemplating how hard things are, how difficult your life is, or how much work you have to do. Monitor your thinking when you socialize and when you spend time alone. Unless you know how you think when you are alone, you will not be able to recognize the effect that others have.

Look out for effects on your emotions, too. You may not feel as if companions affect you emotionally until you take a deeper look. You may feel suddenly tired or you may feel happy and charged with energy. All of the emotions, thoughts, and physical sensations that you have provide valuable information about your whole self.

Body Work
Exercises to enhance physical, mental, and emotional awareness

(The first three of these exercises are adapted from the teachings of Georgi I. Gurdjieff, a White Russian who was concerned with the great adventure of the search for one's Self. The aim of his teachings is self-knowledge and a consequent release of constructive energy.) These exercises are designed to help you set up a 'silent witness' in yourself, not judgmental, just aware. The process is internal – there are no formulas, no panaceas – and it is called The Work.

1. For an entire day, remember to keep both feet on the floor whenever you are standing or sitting. Although the task may seem easy, for most people, making the effort to do something so non-habitual will be somewhat of a shock. This shock helps 'wake you up' to a greater level of awareness.

2. Consciously alter some other physical habit of your own choosing (e.g., for one day, drink nothing but water).

3. For one day, try to be aware of one part of your body, say your left toe, whenever you can. Feel whatever sensations you can in that area – pulsations, tingling, whatever. Write down what you observe.

4. Progressive Muscular Relaxation (PMR) is a technique for becoming more aware of physical tensions and how to let them go. It was developed in the 1920's by Dr. Edmund Jacobsen as a relaxation tool. PMR involves three assumptions. One, you cannot relax your muscles and worry at the same time. Two, we must first experience muscle tension in order to be able to let go of it and deeply relax. Three, once we can

distinguish between tension and relaxation, we can interrupt tension before it has a chance to develop. The technique itself is simple. You tense the muscles in each area of your body, feel the stress and strain, and then release. First, tense the muscles in your right hand, hold the tightness and tension for about five seconds and then let go. Move up through the forearm, upper arm and shoulders. Continue through the body progressively until you have felt and released tension in every part. Without exception, I have found PMR to be an effective relaxation tool for everyone who has learned the technique. What is more, you don't even have to believe in the treatment's efficacy for it to work!

Caution: PMR may be contraindicated for people with histories of high blood pressure, because it requires subjects to momentarily but artificially increase blood pressure as they tense various muscle groups.

*   *   *   *   *

Once we begin to get a sense of the importance of being aware of everything that is happening in our corporeal lives, we may begin to wonder about specific aspects. In other words, when we begin to become more mindful and when we begin to master the techniques of 'letting go' and 'simply observing', we may want to observe certain specific things about ourselves and others. We want to learn to direct our attention. We want to focus on certain aspects of our lives. This process of **focusing** is discussed in the following chapter.

Chapter 2

FOCUS
Directing Attention

The price of freedom is eternal vigilance.
– Patrick Henry

Inattention

What does it mean to be without attention? A state of daydreaming, imagining, or letting the stream of consciousness flow is what many would call inattention. I believe that real inattention is not possible, because awareness continually rests on one object or another, even if only for a fleeting moment. Lack of attention occurs when someone does not attend to whatever the outsider (who may be another personality of the subject) wishes.

Ordinary Attention

Although not the way we normally conceive of attention, ordinary attention also comes and goes without our consent. Giving attention to a matter is not something we actively do but something that happens to us. The choiceless awareness of ordinary attention is passive in that it is simply a reaction to external events or to an internal stream of consciousness. Our everyday concentration jumps from object to object and its intensity wavers from moment to moment. Right now, as you focus on this passage, you can observe for yourself how your attention wanders. Readers can be pulled away from the words on a page by a thousand different associations.

Focused Attention

Maintaining a focus is, in fact, quite extraordinary. The aim is to develop sustained, directed, and active attention. Focused attention may be distinguished from both inattention and ordinary attention. Anyone who attempts to concentrate on an object will find that the focus is difficult to sustain for any length of time. To prove that difficulty to yourself, set a goal of concentrating on the second hand of a clock for a solid five minutes. If you really try to accomplish this feat, I will wager that you find yourself wishing the task to be over before ten seconds have passed. Your mind will start reviewing the many more important things that you could be doing, and wondering why you are spending your time in such an unpleasant, boring way.

Paradoxically, developing an ability to focus is not a willful process. Rather it is more about allowing something to happen. I once wrote a poem about the process and it is included here to illustrate one way to acquire focused attention.

> *Quiet*
> Sitting
> waiting
> quiet and still
> for something to happen.
> Letting life flow
> ease slips into place
>
> I sit
> and listen
> for the movements inside
>
> I hear soft, sure voices
> that bring quiet strength
> to the day.
> – 9/27/89

Myths about Attention

Paying Attention

The more we examine the concept of focusing, the more it becomes clear that 'paying' attention is a real misnomer. Although directing our attention does require an expenditure of energy, the rewards come back manyfold. The process is not a narrowing inward but instead an opening outward to greet objects that inhabit our world. When we have greater command of focus and direction, we are more clearly alive.

Not 'a tension'

Attention does not require a lot of tension. When we are relaxed and open, we can focus on a topic much more effectively than if we were expending a great deal of muscular effort. Screwing up your face in knots does not help to remember a phrase. Pulling your hair out will not help you to return a tennis serve. Biting your nails will not make your presentation any clearer. These are just a few examples of unnecessary tensions that take us away from a focus rather than helping us maintain one.

Attention Involves Judging

Criticizing and evaluating what you attend to can far outweigh the benefits of focusing. Pure observation involves neither judgment nor criticism. Whenever you measure yourself against an outside standard, it is likely that someone will come up short. You may not like how you compare or you may feel that you only have value when you achieve more or perform better.

One of the delightful characteristics of our physical bodies is that no one can truly be compared to another. Each physical entity is unique and beautiful in its own right. Unfortunately, many of us are too busy judging our own bodies against some outside ideal that has no relation to real people with real bodies. We diet to become as thin as the airbrushed and retouched models in magazines and then wonder why we cannot maintain this artificial image of perfection that does not even exist. Tall people slump to appear shorter and short women wear uncomfortable high heels to look taller. The dancer with the powerful leaps frets over a missed turn, while the one who has mastered the art of intricate footwork persists in jumping until (s)he falls. The grass always seems to be greener when we gaze at our physiques with judging eyes. By appreciating the value of our own body type and abilities and, by focusing on strengths rather than imagined flaws, we are better able to appreciate our true worth (which is considerable) as corporeal beings. (For more discussion of body image, see the section in Chapter 10 on *Relating to the Body*.)

Richard Carson, in his delightful book, *Taming Your Gremlin*, describes how to use attention without falling into the evaluation trap. He distinguishes a process that he calls 'simply noticing' from the evaluative process of 'thinking about'. Carson says focused awareness has nothing to do with asking yourself **why** and it has everything to do with observing **how**.

'Thinking about' is an attempt to figure out how you can control yourself and your universe. 'Simply noticing', on the other hand, is what happens when you experience yourself and your surroundings without attempting to change or manipulate anything. 'Thinking about' removes you from the current experience. 'Simply noticing' puts you in contact with it. 'Simply noticing' is more exciting, creative and fun than 'thinking about'. Given the choice at this moment, which do you choose?

Focus in the Midst of Flux

The world around us is constantly changing – nothing is fixed or certain. According to an anonymous epigram, "Everything in the universe is subject to change – and everything is on schedule." Problems can evoke a sense of adventure, a challenge, and a focus for our efforts if we refuse to get lost in the maze of change. Focusing is a tool to keep us 'on the mark'.

In ancient Greece, focus had a spiritual connotation. Christian writers of that era were so cognizant of focus in a spiritual sense that the word we now know as 'sin' could literally be translated from the ancient Greek as 'missing the mark'.

Goal-Setting

One of the trickiest parts of getting what you want out of life is learning to focus on what you really want. Sometimes as soon as I get a clear picture of my goal, I know what path to take to achieve it. Focusing on that goal can be likened to an 'aha!' experience, where clarity clicks in, and an answer to what has previously seemed a confusing puzzle appears.

Discovering what you want in life can be facilitated by setting goals. By working through the process you may find that some of the desires that you thought were goals are not really what you wanted at all. Goal-setting does not mean that you are stuck with your original aims or tied to pursuing them through struggling and pain.

Focusing is a Tool

On the contrary, goal-setting is a tool. Useful goals are important enough to have real value but they need not be taken too seriously. You always have the freedom to revamp goals as much as you want. By all means, if your goals are not serving you, get rid of them. Appropriate aims give a focus and direction for your energy. If so-called goals are causing you suffering, misery, or pain, they are not right for you.

I would like to relate a personal childhood goal that had to be revamped as my interests changed. Ever since I learned to solve equations in grade school, I wanted to teach math in college. After graduating from a prestigious college with a liberal arts degree, I took extra mathematics courses to build up credentials for graduate school. I stubbornly pursued my childhood dream of becoming a mathematics professor until one day I succumbed to a fit of tears following an advanced calculus class. Only then did I discover that I really didn't want to devote my life to a field that I no longer enjoyed. That day I learned that it is important to stick with objectives that help you, but not with ones that do not.

Guidelines for Setting Goals

- *Learn the art of positive self-talk.* Positive self-talk is a technique used in many diverse fields. It is also known as cognitive restructuring by Ellis, cognitive therapy by Beck, and affirmations by Gawain. The concept relies on the phenomenon that we are always talking to ourselves. Usually we tell ourselves how we should feel, what we must want, or how we ought to behave. 'Shoulds', 'musts', and 'ought tos' are all signs of negative talk. Positive talk 'affirms' what we want.
- *Write or think of goals in the present tense.* If you imagine objectives to be realized in the future rather than the now, the mind never gets a chance to picture the goals as actualized.
- *Affirm what you want, not want you don't.* If you focus on what you don't want, chances are that may be the very thing that you attract.
- *Keep affirmations short and simple.* Short, simple statements tend to be clearer. They leave a strong impression on the mind and emotions. Consider the success in recent years of the thirty-second sound bite. Goals that are long, wordy and theoretical often don't mean anything.
- *Keep self-talk non-competitive.* Since you can never get a real hold on what someone else is experiencing, it is not helpful to pin hopes and dreams on comparisons to others. A goal that is based on someone else doesn't really mean anything.
- *Create a belief that you will achieve your aim.* Temporarily suspending doubts allows you to put your full energy into meeting your objectives. However, goals are not meant to contradict your deepest feelings.
- *Do not deny resistance.* Be aware that emotional reactions are giving you important information. Resistance provides something concrete to work against in order to achieve your goals. Resistance can manifest in many ways. You may feel depressed or overwhelmed at the thought of trying to set goals, for example, or you may find yourself talking,

eating, or sleeping too much in order to distract yourself. Or you may hear inner voices telling you that you 'can't' or 'shouldn't' do that or that you 'ought to' be doing something else. These are all ways to avoid getting what you want. It is important not to repress these kinds of experiences, but to pay attention and learn from them. (Note: More information on resistance is provided in the chapter on **weight**, along with exercises to help you experience your resistance on a physical level.)

Sight – A Physiological Focus

Sight is an active process, requiring effort of the muscles that surround our eyes. Eight pairs of eye muscles act as focusing mechanisms and anchors to hold our eyes in place.

Ciliary muscles allow us to concentrate on near or far distances at will. When the ciliary muscles tense, the lens springs into a convex shape for near vision. When they relax, the lens flattens, allowing for distance vision.

Extraocular muscles surrounding the retina focus images on the retina. When there is too much tension in the muscles surrounding the eyes, the extraocular muscles squeeze the eyeball out of its proper shape, making it too long (so that the image is focused in front of the retina) or too short (so that the image is focused behind it). In either case, the image misses the most densely packed light receptors and the picture looks blurry.

Two more sets of muscles exert control on the process of visual focusing. Recti muscles stretch from front to back, and oblique muscles circle the eyeball. If the recti are tight, the eyeball shortens and the image lands behind the retina, causing farsightedness. If the obliques are chronically tense, they squeeze the eyeball into an elongated shape, causing nearsightedness.

Broad or Narrow Points of View

Visual focus can affect perception dramatically. We can observe only a small portion of a scene, filtering out the background. Or we can step back and take a broad look at the landscape. We can keep our gaze fixed and steady, we can let it wander from point to point, or we can let it roam continuously. Each process produces different information and certainly very different feelings and sensations. In this respect, choosing a line of sight parallels the selection of a focus for other kinds of efforts.

Hawks can choose to fly high and take a broad overlook of the scene below. Or these magnificent raptors can narrow their sights to scrutinize a situation for details such as to pinpoint the location of a mouse. Just so, humans can assimilate the big picture, or we can refine our reception of visual, auditory, tactile, olfactory, and gustatory stimuli. For example, we can finely tune our hearing to pick out the special nuances of a musical phrase or a pointed conversation. In either case, it is important to recognize that directing attention is a tool. Changing perspective allows us to gather different types of information. Focusing does not, in and of itself, tell the whole truth.

One Focus does not Reveal the Whole Truth – Seeing a Piece of the Pie

Have you heard the old adage about not being able to 'see the forest for the trees'? Do you remember the story of the five blind men and an elephant? Some say the five men represent the five senses. Each man is led to a different part of the elephant, and all are asked to describe what an elephant is. The first blind man says, "I can tell you what an elephant is. He is very thin with a long shock of hair. He is always moving." The second man says, "No, no, that's not what an elephant is like at all. He **is** thin, but not that thin. You forgot to mention that an elephant is hollow on the inside and he sucks up lots of things and blows other things out of that hollow tube. And you are wrong about the hair. There is no hair; well, maybe a few long bristles." The third jumps in to say, "How can you both be so wrong? An elephant does not move much at all. An elephant is strong and straight; he emerges from the ground like the trunk of a tree." The fourth man claims only he knows the truth. "An elephant is like a huge, gently sloping mound. He is mostly flat, without much demarcation." The last blind man is convinced that everyone else is completely mistaken. "An elephant is large and floppy. He extends up high a long way but has little width. He is always swishing and swirling around flies, so he must really enjoy their company."

Ask yourself now, which one of the blind men is right? In this story, each is absolutely correct about what he perceives, but each one knows only a part of the truth about the elephant. Each individual's focus is so narrowed that no one perceives the big picture.

Movement as a Focusing Tool

When a dancer or an athlete focuses on the mastery of a difficult dance step or routine, (s)he can often tackle and best a problem that, at first, seemed insurmountable. I remember a time when I put a great deal of effort and focus on learning how to perform a cartwheel. As a fresh-faced ninth-grader, I found out that one requirement for the cheerleading tryout was 'one perfectly executed cartwheel on demand'. At that time, I didn't know how to cartwheel, but I wanted very much to become a cheerleader. If I succeeded in this goal, my social life was a guaranteed success. At least that is what I convinced myself to believe. That belief was enough to motivate me to master a skill that I had never mastered before. I practiced and practiced and held in mind the ultimate aim (teenage popularity). Focusing was key – that time, it helped me learn to cartwheel, at other times it helped me learn to drive a car, or ride a bike, or do a pirouette on toe. When the act was important to me and my goal was one-pointed enough, it seemed that I could achieve anything I wanted to do.

Focusing on a physical task can serve as a paradigm for enhancing the ability to focus and refocus productive thoughts and emotions. For instance, many of my college-aged hatha yoga students practice kinesthetic focusing before undertaking an enterprise that requires a lot of concentration (like writing a term paper or studying for finals). The students adopt postures, such as the tree or dancer pose (described in the next chapter's Body Work), that require fixing the attention upon a point and becoming quiet within. These preparatory movements, they claim, help to achieve a clearer focus, which can be applied to studies, work, or anything.

Body Work

(Exercises 2 and 4 have been greatly influenced by the work of Dan Millman, a world champion gymnast who has incorporated his inner and outer trainings to create an approach to life that he calls 'The Way of the Peaceful Warrior'.)

1. *Attention – Not a Tension*
   a) As you are reading this passage, **freeze**. Don't move at all. Pay attention to the position of your body and your body sensations. Can you drop your shoulders? If so, your muscles were unnecessarily lifting them. Can your forearm muscles relax? If so, you were unnecessarily tensing. Can you relax your forehead? If so, you were stressing those muscles for no useful purpose. Check your stomach, thigh, and calf muscles. Are they contracted more than needed?
   b) Now take a moment to concentrate on letting go. Let as many of your muscles relax as possible. Notice the difference.

2. *Focused Attention*
Take a ball and throw it in the air. Staying relaxed and easy, catch it. Now, consider the moment the object was in the air. At that moment, you weren't focused on what errands you had to complete or what you ate for lunch. Other thoughts may have intruded either before you threw the ball or after you caught it, but during the throw, you were pure attention, reaching out, attuning your body to achieve the catch. In that moment, your mind and body were completely alert and you were practicing focused attention.

3. *Hatha yoga asanas that create a change in focus.* Sometimes you can change your perspective just by changing your physical position. Small children instinctively realize this when they are held upside down by an adult. They laugh and squeal with delight. One way to reproduce those feelings in yourself is to suspend yourself from a bar, or to let your head

hang down from the seat of a chair. As blood rushes to your head, you can also feel the rush of strangeness and change. Or you can practice the yoga asanas (poses) described below. These inverted hatha yoga poses will literally turn your world upside down.

a) Shoulder *Stand* (Sarvangasasana) – Lie on the back, place the arms down along the sides of the body with the legs together. Inhaling, slowly raise both legs until they are perpendicular to the floor. Then lift the hips, and then each segment of the spine until only the shoulders rest on the floor. Use the hands to support the back and walk the hands down the vertebrae as you lift first the lower, then middle, then upper spine. Keep the legs straight and together. Breathe evenly and hold for a minute or as long as you can, whichever comes first.

b) Half *Plow* (Ardha halasana) – Lie on the back with legs together and flat on the floor and arms alongside the body with palms on the floor. Inhaling, slowly raise both legs until they are perpendicular to the floor, keeping the legs straight and together. Extend the feet beyond the head until the legs are parallel to the floor. Breathe evenly and hold for ten seconds. Exhaling, slowly lower the hips and return the legs first to the perpendicular position and then back down to the floor.

(Note: *Head Stand* (Shirshasana) – although the head stand is an inverted pose, it is a strenuous posture and should be approached with extreme caution. Even young healthy persons should practice hatha yoga daily for two to three months before attempting the headstand. For that reason it is not described here, and is suggested for use only under the supervision of a skilled hatha yoga instructor.) To be safe, do not attempt any inverted poses without first having them demonstrated and supervised by a skilled and credentialed yoga instructor.

4. *Distracted Attention*
a) Have a friend stand comfortably with hands at the sides. Have the friend tense one arm straight and clench the fist, with the arm pointed down along the side of the body. Tell your partner you

are going to try to pull their arm away from the body, sideways. Do so and notice the amount of effort required for you to pull the arm out.

b) Next, tell your friend that first you are going to zigzag your hand in front of them, then you will try to pull their arm. Do so. Was there a difference in the amount of effort you had to expend when you distracted your partner's attention?

5. *Changing focus – wide vision*

a) We often think of focusing as a process where we narrow in and concentrate all our attention on a small portion of the whole. In this exercise, you are asked to broaden your visual focus. Sense the world as if you were stepping back a little from reality, so that you can encompass more. You might even imagine yourself looking through a pair of glasses or standing behind yourself when viewing your world. This way of relating to reality is called 'wide vision'. What does your world look like when you perceive in this way? How are things different? How are they the same?

b) Apply the concept of wide vision to other senses. For example, what new perspectives about sounds arise when you practice 'wide listening'? What new sensations appear when you open yourself up to 'wide touch'?

6. *Changing focus – eye exercise.* When we get very involved with minute tasks such as reading and writing, muscles around the eyes tend to tighten. This drill, influenced by hatha yoga and Bates eye therapy, is designed to work out strained eye muscles. My students use the movement for 'tired, study eyes' when they have been staring at a book or computer screen for hours on end. It allows the eyes to take a break. Just as your back needs a rest when you sit in the same position for many hours, your eyes need relief from a constant focus. Many claim they actually see better after the visual workout. The world looks clearer and more in focus. Try it for yourself.

Keeping your head still, look up, (only with your eyes) then down and repeat. Look right, then left, and repeat. Now repeat the entire sequence.

Look to the right upper diagonal, then to the left lower diagonal, and repeat. Look to the left upper diagonal, then to the right lower diagonal, and repeat. Now repeat this entire second sequence. Imagine a gigantic clock in front of you and look at the twelve on that clock. (You should be looking directly up, just as you did in the beginning of the exercise.) Look sequentially (moving only the eyes and not the head) at one, two, and three. (At three o'clock, your eyes should be pointing directly to your right.) Continue clockwise to four, five, and six. (At six on the clock, your eyes are pointing directly down.) Now move on to seven, eight, and nine (nine is directly to your left) and on through ten, eleven and back to twelve. Reverse the entire process to go counterclockwise, pausing at each numeral on your imaginary clock. When you reach twelve again, rub your hands together until you feel heat from the friction of the rubbing. When you have built up heat, place the palms over the eyes (with eyes open) and allow the eyes to absorb the heat energy (in Bates terminology, this is known as palming). When the eyes have absorbed all of the energy, remove the palms and look out at the world with fresh, new, revitalized eyes.

*   *   *   *   *

Once we have learned to direct our attention, it is only natural to seek an object to focus upon. In order to anchor that focus, it seems fitting to direct our attention to the body. After all, the general focus for *Bodylessons* is the human body. But every body has many different capabilities worthy of attention. Where shall we start?

I believe it would be most beneficial to begin by getting acquainted with our own bodies, without regard to other people, places, time, or things. One quality that a body can manifest on its own, abstracted from any outside interference, is the way it holds its own structure, the way it stands upon itself. Thus, **posture** is the object of discussion in the next chapter.

Chapter 3

POSTURE
An Attitude of the Body

The greatest discovery of my generation is that
human beings can alter their lives by altering their
attitudes of mind.
– William James

When I hear the word 'posture', the first image that comes to mind is a physical one. I tend to think of posture as the physical alignment of the spine, i.e., the physical alignment of each vertebra upon itself. We know that poor posture can have devastating effects on the functioning of the body. Slumping can cramp the internal organs and make it difficult to breathe, digest, or perform any of the basic metabolic functions that enable us to live. Yet the effects of standing tall are not limited to physiology. A change in posture can significantly affect the intellect and the emotions. The lessons of posture/attitude lead us naturally into an investigation of the interconnections between body alignment and emotions. This chapter's Bodylesson also explores the relationship between physical and intellectual 'posturing'.

Physical Posture

Posture is one of the most fundamental concepts of kinesthetic awareness. To be aware of my posture I need only observe myself as I am alone, abstracted from time or space and without relation to other people, places or things. Each pose is a static phenomenon, a snapshot in time.

Thus, it is an easier endeavor to capture and observe a posture than to isolate other concepts revolving around movement. One can look at a pose as if time and space did not exist. An isolated stance does not involve moving from place to place. Postures are pictures frozen in time. As long as they last, they remain the same. Similarly, posture can be abstracted from weight, from energy, from most of the other Bodylessons that are presented for study in future chapters. And although posture can have a relationship to another person, place or thing (e.g., my feet are facing away from the audience), a single pose need not be considered in relation to anything else in order to be understood.

Physical A-LINE-MENT

A line is the basis of our body structure as the spinal column. The line of the spine has a natural curve. Unnatural sagging such as swayback or stooped shoulders causes excessive curvature accompanied by strain and fatigue.

The spine is truly the 'backbone' of our physical structure. A healthy and flexible spine is a key element in maintaining a healthy and youthful body. The spine rests on the strong cradle of the pelvis and the legs connect the body to the earth. From the support of the spine, the shoulders hang in relaxation without need for holding or strain, and from them the arms are supported without effort. On the top of the spine rests the head, not straining forward or attempting to support itself, just sitting in balance on top of the cervical vertebrae.

There are only two stable positions in gravity. These are horizontal and vertical. If your body is lying flat or standing straight, it is naturally aligned in gravity. However, if the body is out of line because of poor posture, extra energy is required to keep it stable in the pull of gravity. You need to exert muscular effort or lean on a crutch to maintain an out-of-line posture. When you are aligned, not only are all physical parts of the body in line, but the body is attuned with a stable psychological posture as well.

Mental Attitudes

Common usage of the verb, 'to posture', gives a clue to the relationship between attitudes of the body and attitudes of the mind. In the active sense, 'posturing' refers to the psychological stance one takes in reference to an idea or an event. We also use the phrase 'to take a stand', and by that we mean to adopt a certain intellectual point of view. We commonly say one should 'stand up' for what (s)he believes in. 'Standing tall' signifies being confident, and serves as another example of a mental attitude that is shaped by and literally created out of a physical posture. We 'withstand' or weather a hardship, and when things go wrong sometimes we ask 'how can we stand' to bear it?

The American Heritage Dictionary lists several definitions of the term 'attitude', including a mental formulation, an orientation, a disposition, and a state of mind or feeling with regard to some matter. In ballet, an 'attitude' is actually a French term for a specific dance step, in which the dancer stands on one leg with the other bent backwards at the knee and opposite arm raised. In jazz dance, the entire discipline relies on an attitude, a sort of self-assured, quick-stepping, smart presentation of movement. One might even call the jazz attitude a mind game that the dancer uses to 'psych up' for a performance.

In fact, specific and identifiable physical postures can be associated with most movement styles. In ballet, for example, the basic posture is tall and elegant, rigidly stretched with an illusion of fluidity. Tummy and derriere are tucked in and the head is held high. In modern dance, postures are grounded deep in the legs, and the attitude is heavy and wild. In Flamenco or Spanish dance, the body is stretched with pride, with extended arms and strong stomping feet that demonstrate a defiant yet controlled approach to movement.

Cognitive Restructuring – Changing Mental Attitudes

Most events that cause us turmoil do so because of our attitude about the situation. Just as we can consciously shift our physical position, so can we alter our attitude of mind. Cognitive restructuring is a process that allows us to change our interpretation of events, in order to reduce mental, emotional or physical upset. The steps of the process are:

1. *Identify the source of the upset.* Choose an event that seems threatening or emotion-evoking. (Hint: A common occurrence affords plenty of opportunities to practice rethinking its consequences.)

2. *Analyze your original attitude toward the event.* Describe the way that you currently appraise the event. Outline why the event is threatening to you. Immediately following an event, what thoughts run through your mind that cause turmoil? What are you afraid of? What do you fear might happen?

3. *Generate alternative attitudes.* When the event occurs, or immediately afterwards, what other ways could you interpret it besides being a threat or problem? Generate as many alternate perspectives as possible that involve appraising the event as a benign occurrence, challenge or stimulus for growth.

4. *Select a new attitude.* Review your list of alternatives. Which ones truly sound plausible, and which sound phony? Select a thought that is a genuine reinterpretation of what has occurred. Make sure that the thought leads to less mental anguish than your previous interpretation. Otherwise, the exercise is futile, except as an intellectual pursuit.

5. *Try it.* The next time you encounter your selected event, make a deliberate effort to focus on your new, positive attitude. The human mind can only process a limited amount of information at one time. See how replacing the negative attitude with a more positive one impacts on the real-life situation.

6. *Analyze the substitution.* After trying the reappraisal, determine what, if anything, may be working against you. If your new positive attitude seems comfortable, then continue to use it as it stands. If the new view doesn't seem quite right, try to identify why it doesn't fit. You may need to modify your attitude. If so, work through the steps again and repeat the process until you are comfortable with the results.

Let's try to apply the process of cognitive reappraisal to a real life situation, so we can better see how it can work.

Following the outline above, step one would be to choose an event. How about this situation? Let's say that you are out on a first date with an attractive partner and you spill red wine all over yourself. Step two is to analyze your original attitude towards the event. A typical negative attitude might be, "Oh, I'm such a stupid person for spilling the wine. I'm sure no one would be attracted to me." Step three is to generate alternatives. Some other ways that you could interpret the situation might be: "Who else could spill their wine as gracefully as I did?" or "I spilled my wine, but my date made me do it." or "Even though I spilled my wine, I'm still a valuable and worthwhile person." In step four we actually pick one of the alternatives. The first alternative seems a little silly, and the second may engender some antagonism towards my date, so let's go with the third interpretation. After we try out the new appraisal, step five, we implement step six by analyzing how it worked. Those you have to do for yourself. It is likely that on your next date, the new mental attitude may allow you to accept the event and perhaps even laugh.

Emotions and Attitudes

Have you ever felt your body slumped and heavy because of depression or discouragement? And have you ever attempted to straighten your spine and lighten your stance, only to discover that in fact, you no longer felt discouraged or depressed, but hopeful, courageous, even joyful – that changing your posture was like lifting a heavy veil to make everything brighter? Then you have experienced the interconnectedness of physical and emotional attitudes.

When we are shocked or frightened, typically the shoulders respond by rising up or by hunching over in a protective crouch. This is much the same way as a pet cat responds by arching his back when he feels threatened. Normally an event that creates fear will eventually resolve itself in a way that we can accept. When that kind of resolution occurs we allow ourselves to relax and resume a neutral, unfrightened body posture.

But sometimes fear is never fully resolved, and the shoulders remain in an arched and rigid posture long after the immediate danger has passed. When this happens, fear becomes internalized and the experience of fright actually becomes locked into the structure of the body.

You can see for yourself how corporeal attitudes can reflect mental and emotional responses to current situations and even events that have long passed. To begin the investigation, use your body to demonstrate a variety of emotional feelings, such as happiness, fear, anger, or pride. Allow your body to express these feelings through changes in posture. As you assume each psychological pose, pay attention to the information revealed by the positioning of the shoulders, head, stomach, legs, and arms. After your body has taken on these various feelings, let the shoulders settle back into their customary position. Do you recognize any of the feelings you tried on earlier? Now let the lower back return to its habitual position. Does it feel at home in any of the attitudes you artificially assumed? Continue isolating other parts of the body and comparing habitual postures with your new repertoire of poses.

Dychtwald suggests using the shoulders as the main focus for this exercise because they are easily adaptable to a variety of readily noticeable shapes and positions. The head is another area that often reveals the emotional state of the body, and may belie verbal attempts to hide true feelings.

Body Work
Part I – Increasing Awareness of Your Posture

1. When you begin to examine your posture, it may be useful at first to use a mirror to locate slouches and slumps, tensions, and stress. But do not depend on the mirror so much that it becomes a crutch. You want to be able to feel the stresses and strains in your body, so that you can adjust and correct them anytime, not just when you are in front of the looking glass.

For me, I can feel how my shoulders and neck collect a large percentage of the tensions on any given day. If I am out in heavy traffic, or feeling impatient while waiting in line, or if anything the least bit stressful occurs, it is not long before I feel my shoulders creeping up, up, up. Before I know it, my shoulders are almost touching my ears, and my neck seems to have disappeared altogether.

Another place where worries and cares tend to settle is in the derriere. Constantly contracted gluteal muscles can be very uncomfortable, even painful. Some of you who have taken dance or aerobics classes may have been told to "Tighten up those buttocks! Tuck in!" For those people, let me interject one note of warning . . . don't! When you tighten and hold any muscle unnaturally, you clutch tensions inside rather than allowing them to slip away. The spinal column normally forms a soft, flowing 'S' curve. Tucking in the derriere abbreviates the 'S' and thrusts out your tummy into an unnatural, unsightly, and unhealthy 'C'.

Some students in my dance or yoga classes, when told to stand tall, jerk themselves up suddenly, locking their knees. Locked knees are the result of crunching the patella (knee bone) so far back in its socket that it can no longer move. If you are chronically pushing your knees back against the direction that they normally bend, you are creating this syndrome. Bending the knees a little will free you from the uncomfortable and unnatural locked knee position.

A 'frozen face' appears on many people who are trying very hard to stand erect. For that matter, the frozen face is often the hallmark of people who are trying very hard to do anything. But all that concentration and effort that lodges in the face in unnecessary. Once your body learns how, it will hold a graceful and easy pose all by itself. Squinting and screwing up your nose will not help at all, whether you are trying to build a good posture, investigate a new movement, or study for an upcoming exam.

2. Try maintaining a tall, stretched, elegant and erect posture continuously for five minutes at a time. During this period, keep your back long, your chin gently tucked in, your shoulders relaxed, and the back of your head stretched upward. How do you feel? What thoughts entered your mind (if any) as you tried on the elegant pose?

3. Experience your building blocks askew as you 'slump'. Feel the discomfort and muscle strain. When the stable, strong, yet flexible structure of the spine is habitually misaligned in this way, your muscles must take up the slack and do double duty in supporting your body. A natural function of the bones becomes a chronic strain for the muscles.

Stand up, then lean slightly forwards, sideways, or backwards from the waist. Do you feel a pressure or slight tension in your muscles as they now exert an extra effort to hold you up? If you were to hold this unnatural position for any length of time, even two minutes, it would soon become painful. The pain is a result of all the contortions the rest of your body must make to maintain the poor posture.

4. The practice of Hatha Yoga can help improved posture. To begin this study of the spine, lie on your back with knees raised and the soles of the feet on the floor. Press the entire spine to the floor. Clasp your knees to the chest, pressing the knees close to your chest in the Wind-Releasing Pose (pavanamuktasana). Feel your lower back against the floor. Now relax both legs to the floor and lie still, keeping the lumbar area (lower back) as close to the floor as possible.

Press your neck toward the floor. The neck won't actually touch, but aim towards that position in the effort to feel the fully aligned spine from the coccyx (tailbone) through the cervical vertebrae (neck).

Clasp both hands under your head. Tug the neck gently up. Lower your head again to the floor. Now tug up diagonally to each side, without turning your head from side to side.

After this stretch of your neck muscles, relax on your back for a moment, then begin to raise your upper chest from the sternum in the Half-Fish Pose (ardha matsyasama). Imagine a string pulling you up from the sternum (breastbone), until the top of your head rests on the floor. Return to the floor by curling down from the bottom of the spine.

5. Isolations are just what they sound like. The idea is to isolate one part of the body and move only that specific part. Isolations allow you to study the postures of your different body parts as if each were a whole in itself. To begin, put on some favorite music and move your head to the beat. Don't move anything else! The head can go from side to side, up and down, diagonal, in circles; any movement that is comfortable is fair game. Then work the shoulders, chest and rib cage, hips (my favorite!), legs and feet. Play with the music and have fun expressing different bodily attitudes with the isolations.

Part II – Exercises to improve the effectiveness and healthiness of your posture

6. Once I become aware of all the tight spots where my worries and anxieties tend to gather, I find it useful to literally 'build' a healthy posture from the ground up. The following exercise is designed to help you do the same. Sitting on the floor, start with the feet a comfortable width apart, knees bent, and fingertips resting on the floor. Let the head relax and fall forward. Slowly, very slowly, roll your body upwards into an erect position, vertebra by vertebra by vertebra. As you roll up, feel the stable support of the pelvis and the bones of the spine rising from the pelvic girdle. Feel the natural building blocks of your vertebrae in alignment. Sense how each vertebra builds upon what has gone before. Balance the head easily on top of the spinal sculpture; wear it as a confident crown. There is no need for a 'military posture', but simply a relaxed reliance on the strength of the bony skeleton. Once you have unfolded and are standing comfortably erect, then, if you wish, look in the mirror. Looking back will be someone with a healthier posture – a more appealing, happier you.

7. The constant pull of gravity can be debilitating on the body. Every day your vertebrae are compressed against one another with only small cushions (discs) between them. Your feet bear a tremendous amount of weight; the entire mass of the body presses down on them. To combat this crunch, it helps to hang.

   a) Grab hold of any hanging bar that will support your weight (e.g., a chin-up bar would be an excellent choice). Hang for ten seconds. Feel the joints open and the spine stretch out.

   b) If you do not feel comfortable hanging from a bar, perhaps you will want to try this adapted version. Find a comfortable, cushiony chair, and place your back on its seat with your legs draped over the back of the chair. Let your head hang down from the chair and feel your cervical vertebrae open up and out. What is the effect on your posture and attitude after just a few minutes of this therapy?

*   *   *   *   *

Now that you have studied the basic structure of the body, you may want to examine qualities that manifest themselves through this fundamental form. One characteristic of the human body that I find most fascinating is its ability to be flexible, to adapt to new situations. Flexibility is shared to some degree by all living things, and it is that which allows us to grow. Continue on to Chapter 4 to learn more about **flexibility**.

Chapter 4

FLEXIBILITY
The Ability to Adapt and Grow

It is not fair to ask of others what you are not willing
to ask of yourself.
– Eleanor Roosevelt

To be what we are, and to become what we are capable
of becoming, is the only end in life.
– Robert Louis Stevenson

Corbin and Lindsey describe flexibility as the range of motion available in a joint. Just as a physically fit person can move the body through a whole range of motion in work and at play, a psychically fit person can move into a wide variety of situations with ease and grace.

Adaptability

When we say that someone is physically flexible, we generally mean that (s)he is able to adapt easily to new physical positions without too much stress or strain. The word, 'flexibility', can be used in a similar way to describe psychological adaptation. When we say that someone is flexible, we generally mean that (s)he is able to 'roll with the punches', so to speak. A flex'able' person can adapt more readily to new situations without much psychological stress or emotional strain.

Reichian Theory – Physical Manifestations of Psychological Inflexibility

Dr. Wilhelm Reich, a controversial psychoanalyst who studied under Sigmund Freud, was one of the first theoreticians to talk about the relationship between tension and rigidity in the body and rigidity or psychological limitations in the mind. When emotions are held in rather than expressed, they affect the musculature of the body. When the body is tense, perceptions are locked in. Reich believed that emotions are a form of energy. If they overwhelm us, we may tense our muscles to stem the flow of feeling. A one-time muscular defense can lead to chronic tension when we continue to suppress the emotion behind the tightness.

Reich discovered that groups of muscles in the body tend to form protective armor. Segments of the body that are prone to armoring are the eye area, around the mouth, the neck, thorax, diaphragm, abdomen and pelvic areas. The armor blocks bodily energy, which Reich called orgone. In Reichian therapy (and its offshoots, Bioenergetics and Radix) body armor is softened and removed gradually through combinations of physical manipulation, movement, and/or psychoanalysis.

Stretching and Growth

Adaptability is not the only advantage that arises from studying and practicing the Bodylesson of flexibility. To become more flexible, we need to stretch. Quite literally, stretching means to reach further, beyond, and past the customary tasks that we are used to performing. Stretching means enlarging our comfort range so that we are more able and more capable. The result is that we become more powerful and more human than we were before we made the extra effort. In other words, the natural result of stretching is that we 'grow'.

Within its capacity, a human organism will adapt to demands placed upon it. Learning is one kind of adaptation, physical stretching and reaching is another kind of growth. All living things and some non-living things adapt – even rocks adapt. If you grind a rock with a tool, it will naturally adapt by changing shape. But the change that results from practicing Bodylessons is not simply a matter of adding on or taking away more of the same thing. More than a quantitative variation, experiential growth involves qualitative change, i.e., a fundamental change in kind.

When we 'stretch', we are trying out new positions and roles that may be uncomfortable at first. With commitment and persistence, our flexibility inevitably improves, and we become more comfortable with new challenges and situations. The process is cyclical. Subsequently, we become more open to future challenges that require us to reach further still – perhaps further than we ever believed possible.

Improved flexibility has many intermediate benefits that in themselves contribute to improved adaptability and long-term growth. Two important intermediate rewards are an increased resistance to stress and enhanced body awareness.

Resistance to Stress

Professional athletes and trainers have long known that what you do before and after exercising is just as important as what you do while you exercise. Physical stretching is an important bridge between the sedentary and the active life. It prepares you for movement and helps you make the daily transition from inactivity to vigorous activity without undue strain. It is especially important if you engage in strenuous exercises like running, cycling, or tennis, because these activities promote tightness and inflexibility. Warm-up and cool-down periods with gentle stretching should be included before and after workouts or any strenuous activity. Stretching reduces muscle tension and increases relaxed movement. In turn, freer and easier movements improve motor coordination, so you perform better at sports. Warm-up, stretching, and cool-down should each take about five to ten minutes, a total of fifteen to thirty minutes that may make the difference between efficient and inefficient, or even harmful exercise.

Stretching before and after workouts will help prevent injuries. Some sports injuries are so common that they have special colorful nicknames. Shin splints, whiplash (neck strain) and charley horse (arm or leg strain) are some of these. If you keep bending a wire back and forth, it will break at the weakest point. Similarly, if you force a joint that is stiff, you will damage it. Sprains imply trauma to either the ligaments (the bands connecting bones) or other soft tissues of a joint. Strains or muscle pulls occur when muscles or their tendon attachments are stretched to the point where their fibers actually start to tear. Effective motion always requires a balance of suppleness and strength. The more flexible you are, the less energy you need to expend in order to move the body and the less likely you are to hurt yourself.

Increased Body Awareness

Developing flexibility also develops body awareness. As you stretch various parts of the body, you feel where they are tight or relaxed, where they hurt and where they are free. Those sensations allow you to focus in on the needs of your body, and to notice its peculiarities (e.g., "My body feels stiff before lunch," or, "It feels sluggish after dinner."). Listening and responding to your body's signals helps the body move for its own sake rather than for reasons of competition or ego. Stretching promotes circulation, thereby oxygenating and waking up every cell in the body. And, most importantly, stretching feels good.

When to Stretch

One of the great things about stretching is that it can be done anytime and anywhere you feel like doing it. Certainly, stretch before and after physical activity, but also stretch at various times of the day when you can. Perhaps you would enjoy lengthening your body in the morning before the start of the day. Or maybe it would be more convenient to stretch at the office to release nervous tension. Some other suggestions include after sitting or standing for long periods of time, whenever you feel stiff, or during 'downtimes' (e.g., while waiting in line or watching television).

How to Stretch

According to Bob Anderson in his book, *Stretching*, it should feel good. You do not have to push yourself to the limit or attempt to go further each day. It should not be a personal contest to see how far you can go. Stretching should be tailored to your particular muscular structure, flexibility and varying tension levels. The keys are regularity and relaxation. Without even working at it, you naturally become more supple when you are relaxed, on vacation, or free from prevailing problems and concerns. The object of stretching is to gently open and free up all of the joints, in order to increase your ease of movement and to extend your range of power – not to concentrate on attaining extreme flexibility, which can lead to overstretching and injury.

Many of the hatha yoga exercises take their names from the natural movements of animals (e.g., lion, crocodile, cat, fish, cobra, scorpion). We, too, can learn more about how to stretch by observing the neighborhood creatures. Animals instinctively know how to elongate their muscles; they do so spontaneously, never straining but continually and naturally tuning up muscles that they are preparing to use.

The right way to stretch is a relaxed, sustained (static) stretch with attention focused on the muscles that are being lengthened. The wrong way is to bounce up and down (ballistic movements) or to extend to the point of pain. These methods can actually do more harm than good.

When you begin, spend ten to thirty seconds in the 'easy stretch'. Go to a point where you feel a mild tension, and relax as you hold the stretch. The feeling of tension should subside as you hold the position. If it does not, ease off slightly.

Then progress to the 'developmental stretch'. To do this, increase your stretch (only a tiny amount – probably by only a fraction of an inch) until you again feel a mild tension and hold for ten to thirty seconds. The tension should diminish. If not, ease off a little.

Avoiding the Stretch Reflex

Your muscles are protected by a mechanism called the 'stretch reflex'. Any time you pull muscle fibers too far (e.g., by bouncing or overextending yourself), a nerve reflex responds by sending a signal to the muscles to contract. This keeps the muscles from being injured. When you stretch too far, you tighten the very muscles you are trying to flex. The reflex is similar to the involuntary muscle reaction that takes place when you accidentally touch a hot stove; without thinking your body pulls away from the heat.

Holding a stretch as far as you can push it or bouncing up and down strains the muscles and activates the stretch reflex. These harmful methods cause pain as well as physical damage due to the microscopic tearing of muscle fibers. This tearing leads to formation of scar tissue in the muscles, with a gradual loss of elasticity. Torn and scarred muscles become tight and sore.

Without movement, bodies tend to lose their flexibility over time. Muscles contract and become tight unless they are challenged. Before the age of eighteen, we do not need to stretch to maintain suppleness. After that, we need to sustain a pose for at least eight to ten seconds just to maintain the flexibility we already have. To increase our range of motion, we must sustain a posture for at least one full minute.

Guidelines

The following guidelines can help you to coax your body into a more flexible state. From this state, enhanced adaptability and openness to growth may arise.

- Remember that *you are the expert* when it comes to determining your stretching needs. You know better than anyone else exactly where, when, and just how much your body needs to loosen up to accomplish what you ask it to do. No one else can feel this as well as you.
- *Relax into the stretches.* Whenever you feel tight, first sense the places

where you are tense (e.g., neck, or lower back, or behind the knees). Then **let go** of the tension, breathe deeply and imagine the breath going to the tight area, loosening it.

- *Stretching should feel good.* Many of us incorrectly learned to associate pain with physical improvement and were taught that the more it hurts, the better. That 'no pain, no gain' adage is a myth. Pain is an indication that something is **wrong**. Listen to your body's signals. A sharp acute pain is a warning bell to immediately stop what you are doing to cause the pain and pain that does not go away (after more than four to five days) is a cue to seek medical advice.
- *Stretch when the body is warm.* It is easier, it feels better, and it does you more good. Cold stretching hurts more and creates a greater opportunity to tear muscles.
- Stretch only a little each time you stretch, but *do it often.* Three or four minutes of relaxed stretching twice a day is better than 15 minutes of grinding and groaning.
- *Don't bounce*!!!!

Body Work

Every part of the body could benefit from increased suppleness and resiliency, but some areas tend to hold on to tightness more than others. For that reason, exercises for these special areas are provided first.

1. Neck and Shoulders. Begin with some easy stretches for the neck. Let the head fall forward, and feel a slight tension as you hold the position for ten seconds. Slowly and easily let the head move to the right so that your right ear is close to your shoulder. Hold for ten seconds. Just as gently, lift the head up and back so that the chin is pointing towards the ceiling. (Do not allow the head to flop back on the neck. Flopping invites injury. The neck should feel lifted and graceful, not shortened and weak.) Hold for ten seconds. Move the head so that the left ear is close to your shoulder. Hold. Repeat the four points in the reverse direction.

Shoulder Shrugs are just what they sound like. Bring the shoulders up close to the ears and hold them there. Feel the shrug squeezing out the tension. Repeat several times and then move into slow rolls forward, up, back, and down. Reverse the circles so that the shoulders are moving back first, then up, forward, and down.

2. Lower back stretch. This is a particularly good stretch to do before any kind of heavy labor, especially in the morning or when the weather is cold. By protecting the muscles in the lower back, you can prevent many injuries. Stand with feet about shoulder-width apart and pointed straight ahead. Slowly bend forward from the hips. Keep the knees slightly bent so that the lower back is not stressed. Let your neck and arms relax. Go to the point where you feel a slight stretch in the back of your legs. Hold this pose until you can relax into it. Mentally concentrate on the area being lengthened. Do not lock the knees or bounce. You may be able to touch your toes or just above the ankles – wherever you touch is fine. Return slowly to a standing position.

3. Calf Stretch. Face a wall, or something else that you can lean on for support. Step back and rest your forearms on the wall and let your head rest on the back of your hands. Now bend one knee and bring it towards the support. The back foot is straight with the foot flat and pointed straight ahead or slightly in. Now, without changing the position of your feet, slowly move your hips forward as you keep the back leg straight and your back foot flat on the floor. Go to an easy stretch in your gastrocnemius (calf muscle). Hold for ten seconds, then move into a developmental stretch and hold for ten seconds more.

4. Back and Hamstring stretch. Lie on your back with both legs bent and feet resting flat on the floor. From this position, lift one leg to a vertical position (or past vertical, if that feels good to you), holding on to the leg with your hands. Make sure that your lower back muscles remain flat on the floor, don't allow the back to do the work. Flex the knee and the ankle and let the leg relax towards the chest. Now straighten the leg and allow it to stretch farther this time. Release and flex the knee and ankle again, then stretch even farther. Now hold this position (eight to ten seconds to maintain what flexibility you have already attained, a full minute to enhance your mobility). Relax, take a deep breath, and repeat on the other side. You may wish to hold a towel in both hands and hook

it over the foot you are stretching if you are not very flexible to start. Remember to keep the straight leg straight. Sacrifice elevation for straightness. Proper position is important to make sure you are working the muscles you want to be stretching.

5. Ability stretch. Choose a physical action that is presently a little beyond your reach. It may be a push up, a sit up, a handstand or anything that you cannot do now. Once you've chosen your feat, attempt to perform it several times in the morning and again in the evening. Do this every day! With each attempt you are asking your body to change. Set no strict performance goals, no time limits, and no specific number of repetitions you must do each day. Continue this for a month and see what happens. Without really trying, you will find your body complying. This strategy can be applied any change you would like to make in your life. It just takes some time and persistence.

6. Psychological stretch. (This kinesthetic demonstration was inspired by the gentle exercises of Moshe Feldenkrais.
   a) Interlace the fingers of both hands. Notice which thumb lands on top. Is it the right thumb, or is it the left? For every person that winds up with a right thumb on top, there is probably a person somewhere in the world who prefers the left. Ask yourself which is the correct way – that is, which hand should be on top? Of course, the answer is that either side can be considered the correct thumb to be on top.
   b) In the second part of this exercise, exchange all your fingers, so that the opposite thumb is on top. Ask yourself how this feels. Does it feel awkward? If you are sharing your experience with other people, consider that probably half of them would find this way of interlacing their fingers (which happens to be so uncomfortable for you) to be comfortable. In this instance, are you willing to give others permission to be different from you? Or are you dogmatic about doing a task the 'right' way, meaning 'your' way?
   c) Continue to hold your hands laced in this unusual (for you) way. After about five minutes you may notice that what once seemed

awkward and uncomfortable now has become a new position that you have made your own.

The psychological stretch can serve as an analogy to many of life's experiences. By trying something new, by doing something in a way you might not have thought of before, you have experienced two important lessons. First, whatever your way of doing things, there is always someone who can come up with a different (and equally effective) method. Second, when you take the risk and try something new, after a while, that new way of adapting becomes incorporated into your repertoire. The willingness to adapt increases your options for coping with any situation.

In many life experiences it is only by being uncomfort-able – by being willing to risk – that you can grow. Think back to the first time you drove a car or went out on a date, or the first time you kissed. These were uncomfortable moments when you were able to expand your growth exponentially. Why? Because you dared to be flexible – you dared to try something new.

*   *   *   *   *

Once we begin to expand ourselves physically (and psychically), it is only natural to peek out from our physical shells and to wonder about everything outside. It is almost as if we were little chicks hatching out into a new and magical world.

Outside we see an environment that will shape how we grow and how we live. Two of the most fundamental characteristics of the environment are **time** and **space**. Our physical bodies and all of our actions take place and are defined in four dimensions (the three dimensions of space: height, width, and length, and the fourth dimensional coordinate of time). For these reasons, let us now turn our attention to the dual Bodylessons of Chapter 5, **time** and **space**.

Chapter 5

TIME and SPACE

Be here now
– Ram Das

*"Well in **our** country," said Alice, still panting a little*
"you'd generally get to somewhere else if you ran very
fast for a long time as we've been doing." "A slow sort
*of country!" said the Queen. "Now **here**, you see, it*
takes all the running you can do, to keep in the same
place. If you want to get somewhere else, you must run
at least twice as fast as that!"
– Lewis Carroll

We live our physical lives within confines of time and space. Each moment in our lives is, was, or will be a 'now'. Past and future moments have become a 'then'. Each place that the physical body inhabits becomes a 'here'. And we describe each place that it was or will be as a 'there'.

Like life, movement can only exist when there is both time and space. Movement is the only artistic form that takes its shape within four dimensions. Without both mediums of time and space, the dancer cannot experience movement nor can (s)he create it. Neither can a spectator view a movement performance outside of space and time.

These boundaries are not the same for other artistic mediums. Graphic arts, for example, produce creations with form and wonderful variations in color, line, and texture. Visual creations live in either two dimensions (e.g., drawings, etching, photographs, and paintings) or three (e.g., sculpture and some collage). They exist in a space. But completed drawings, paintings and sculpture are essentially outside of time. Physically they remain the same; they are always there. Once created, an art object remains essentially the same from one moment to the next. Conversely, music exists in time, but outside of space. The form of a musical piece is composed of varying melodies and rhythms (patterns of sounds) that take shape within a framework of time. Without time, music could not exist, save for a constant tone of a given pitch. Works of literature, when spoken aloud, such as lyrical or epic poems, might also be said to live in time, but not space. Written works, when not orally performed, are the same. Although the physical book exists in a space, it means nothing until we unfold it and read. This, too, takes time.

In fact, even though all of the arts can elicit imaginations that seem to operate in time and space, only the movement arts actually come alive through both mediums. For this reason, it would be helpful to turn to the experience of movement to help solidify observations about time and space.

But before we do, let us take note of a striking dialectic quality shared by concepts of space and time. Both concepts can be viewed alternately as a resource to be used up, or as a process/potential. The first perspective of finititude allows us to deal with time and space as limited entities. The second permits us to imagine them as infinite dimensions. Both points of view have validity in our physical lives, as you will soon see.

Let us now turn to a conceptual and kinesthetic investigation of the nature of time.

TIME

It is difficult to conceive of time, possibly because you cannot physically feel, touch, smell, hear, or taste it. The image most commonly used to portray time is a timeline – a finite structure with a definite beginning and a definite end.

Time as a Finite Resource

Given the concept of time as a finite resource, we are always looking to make the most of the time that we have. How often have you heard the expression, "There just aren't enough hours in the day." We are looking for a way to increase our resource.

Optimal Use of Time – Time Management

Time management techniques do not change the amount of time we have, they merely help us to use the resource more efficiently. Time management may conjure up a notion of a rigid efficiency system where every minute of the day is scheduled and there is no room for error. If so, think again. First, time management involves little more than a collection of simple, easily implemented, and powerful ideas to help you manage your time. Second, 'down time', time to 'goof-off', or relaxation time is built into the system. Human beings are not supposed to work all of the time. Third, time management techniques are suggestions, not prescriptions for a new life. Use options that are workable for you and discard the rest.

Guidelines for Effective Time Management

Some techniques that I have found to be particularly helpful follow. Remember, adopt only the suggestions that feel right to you.

- *Plan your use of time.* Make lists. You can make lists of things to do today, this week, or this month. Pick the time span that works best for you.
- *Prioritize.* Decide what is most important and what can wait. Use the ABC method. For all the items on your list mark them either with an A, B, or C. A's are things you 'must do'. Doing them is a matter of life and death. B's are things that it would be 'good to do' and C's are things that you 'could do' if you had the time. Reassign all the B's to either A or C and cross off all the C's.
- *Do tasks when you are best at them.* Choose morning or night, Monday, midweek or weekend.
- *Learn to say no* to demands on your time.

- *Schedule special times* for phone calls, for visiting, and for doing reports. Otherwise avoid interruptions by disconnecting the phone or limiting time for visitors.
- Learn to *delegate* and ask for help.
- *Break overwhelming jobs into manageable parts.*
- Use the '*once over*'. When you pick up a piece of paper do something with it, even if it is only marking a note on the corner. For things that you have no more use for, use your 'circular file' or trash can. The fewer papers you have to plow through, the more time you save.

Time as a Process

Up to now, we have been conceptualizing time as a finite line, with a definite beginning and end. However, with a little shift in perspective we perceive how any line is comprised of an infinite number of points, an endless row of 'nows'. By altering our point of view, time becomes a process, rather than a product. Studying movements as they occur, in the 'now', can foster this new outlook on time.

Guidelines for Living in the Moment

Some suggestions to help you work on increasing your enjoyment of 'now' are listed here.

- For fifteen minutes recall pleasant memories.
- Don't wear a watch.
- Find a long line to wait in at the supermarket or the bank, and wait in it. When you are ready to strangle the checker or the teller, ask yourself why you are so boring to be with.
- Do absolutely nothing but think about past accomplishments for fifteen minutes.
- Listen to music you enjoy for fifteen minutes.
- Walk, talk or eat more slowly.

- Carefully examine a tree, a flower, sunset, or dawn.
- Tape a mealtime conversation, then play back the tape to see whether you interrupt or talk too fast.
- Read the poem below and reflect upon its meaning.

> *Point of Power*
> Did you ever realize your point of power?
> Like a star
> Your light shines
> and rains
> Energy and fiery brightness.
>
> What a strange paradox –
> How can a tiny speck
> be so massive and so huge
> in its presence?
>
> You are the Point
> The point is the Moment
> and the moment is **now**.
>   – 10/23/89

Movement in Time – Descriptive Variables

Motion through time can be described by several variables which, in themselves, can be manipulated, controlled, and examined. We will discuss three of these – length, tempo, and rhythm.

Length refers to the amount of time it takes to perform a motion or series of motions *in toto*. Length is the interval that is filled (or left unfilled) with movement. An activity that is completed in sixty seconds evokes a completely different feeling than a performance that fills up a period of several hours. A minute waltz, for example, creates a very different sensation from a four-hour Mozart opera extravaganza.

Tempo refers to the relative speed or velocity of the piece – how fast or how slow the movements are. The same activity or gesture can have a very different quality depending on the speed with which it is carried out. Lowering the hand in slow motion is quite different from dropping it with a swift, downward slice.

Rhythm is involved intricately with the number of beats that occur in a given amount of time. Rhythms can be constant or variable, staccato or fluid, syncopated or regular. Rhythms are the patterns we make by breaking up the time. One of our most familiar rhythms is our own heart-beat, our own pulse.

A pulse is a sign of life. It is also a measure of the passing of time. A pulse is the steady cadence that underlies our most familiar movements, such as walking and running, and most of the music we hear. It is also a dancer's and athlete's tool, to keep in synch with other players.

Tap Dance

Tap is the dance medium that most obviously uses, accentuates and plays with time. Using flaps, stomps, brushes, and shuffles, the feet of a tap dancer are instruments that pound out the measure and shape the length, tempo, and rhythm of a piece. Syncopation, sounding a beat out of the expected pattern, is a major tool in tap dance. A tapper can tap out a new cadence in response to a tune, (s)he can make variations on the new rhythm, and (s)he can even modify variations on the variations, if (s)he so desires. In a similar way, at certain points in our lives, we may want to metaphorically dance to new rhythms – to march to 'the beat of a different drummer'.

Body Work – Time

The exercises that follow develop a sense of the rhythm of one's physical, emotional and mental life and an awareness of shaping time.

1. *Human Rhythms*

Part I: *The Pulse*
Measure out your own living rhythm by timing your heartbeat, by feeling your own pulse. To do this, place the first three fingers of your dominant hand (the one you usually write with) on the Adam's apple of your

neck. Simply slide your fingers over on your neck to the dominant side, until you feel the indentation in your neck. Rest your fingers (not your thumb) there. Since your thumb has its own pulse rhythm, you will get a more accurate measure with the fingers. The indentation in the neck is the area where you can best feel the flow of blood in your carotid artery. The carotid is the artery that carries blood from the heart directly to the brain, and it is the place where your own natural pulse is strongest.

Part II: *The Breath*
Get a sense of the rhythm and tempo of your own breathing. How many breaths do you take per minute? Do inhalations take the same amount of time as exhalations?

Continue to monitor your breathing at regular intervals over the course of a week. Are there times when your breathing speeds up? What situations are you in when this happens?

Consciously slow down your rate of respiration. Does this have an effect on how you are thinking or feeling? How so?

Part III: *Observe and Compare*
Measure pulse and respiration rate on a partner. Feel their pulse and watch for breaths. Then reverse roles. It may be interesting to reflect on the effect that you, as the observer, may have on the metabolism of your partner. Does their heart seem to beat faster than yours did when you measured it for yourself? Is their breathing quicker and shallower than your own, or vice versa? Is there a noticeable difference between the pulse (and/or breathing) rate you measured on yourself, and the rate(s) your friend measured for you? If you notice any differences, what could explain them?

2. *The musical pulse*
You can feel a pulse by clapping along in unison, snapping fingers, stomping or using any repetitive motion or sound that mimics a musical beat.
    a) Find a piece of music that you enjoy and sense the pulse by clapping, snapping your fingers or tapping your feet.
    b) In a group of at least three people, put on a tune and find a way to express the beat. Everyone makes the same sound or motion at first.
    c) Now have each member of the group make a different repetitive motion or sound. That becomes your 'personal pulse'.

d) Play out the personal pulses in a round (i.e., one person claps their personal pulse, then the next snaps their personal pulse, and so forth). Can you hold on to your own beat when other sounds (or sights) are going on all around you? How does it feel when you lose your timing? How does it feel when you adopt the rhythm of another?

3. *Tempo*

Perform some task that you do everyday, such as washing the dishes or walking to work, but change your internal velocity while you do it. One way to change your speed setting is to do everything slightly faster than you are used to. Or you can pace yourself slightly slower. Whether you choose to speed up or slow down, you will probably notice how uncomfortable it feels. This is because you have settled into a habitual tempo for any given task. Do you notice how your body, mind, and emotions rebel when you attempt to change internal speeds? The mind says, "This is too fast. I am going to wear myself out." The body says, "I am not comfortable going so slow." The emotions say, "I hate this speed." Are we so habitual, so mechanical that we cannot bear to change velocity, even for a little while?

4. The Last One Wins Race – This game is a variation on the previous lesson. The advantage is that you can play with friends. Competitors begin on a starting line marked about five yards from the finish. On a signal, 'runners' move forward continuously in a direct line to the finish. Each step must be at least ten inches long. The winner is the one who reaches the finish last.

SPACE

Like time, space is a medium that continually surrounds and shapes our journey through physical life. Yet we cannot see, smell, taste, or touch an entity called space. Still, as is true with time, the way that we operate in space defines us as material beings.

Corporeal bodies take up space. Human beings cannot continue to be, without being in some place. At any given moment in time, we exist at an address with definite coordinates in space.

Feng Shui – Optimal Placement

Feng shui is an ancient Chinese practice based on the idea that the auspicious placement of objects in space can bring good fortune. For centuries, the Chinese have believed that if you change your surroundings, you can change your life. Feng shui advocates maintain that proper arrangement of buildings, doors, and other constructions lets energy (chi) flow freely through a structure, creates a healthier environment, facilitates communication, and attracts good luck. A feng shui consultant considers the shape of the building and its physical surroundings, then offers advice on everything from the placement of windows to the positioning of symbolic ornaments on tables. Many of us practice feng shui without knowing it. We instinctively prefer to build houses near a view of rocks overlooking water or to soften the edges of a room with a potted plant. All of us have entered places where we felt immediately comfortable or uncomfortable without being able to explain why.

Space as Potential

We aren't always so fortunate as to live out our lives in perfectly planned spaces, where everything (including you) has its singular perfect ideal place and cannot be moved. Lucky for us. Who would want to live in such a static unchanging space? A dynamic model to describe the way we deal with placement is often a more reasonable alternative than the feng shui ideal. Once again we turn to movement for guidance.

Actualizing the Available Space

As far as a performer is concerned, space is whatever area is available for action. In planned events, the boundaries (e.g., a soccer field, an opera stage) are defined in advance. In a performance, the available movement space is limited by the edges of the playing field or by the stage itself. Space on a stage can be further defined by placing props and lighting strategically throughout. In improvisation, you must make do with whatever space is available at the moment. Movements are the primary designs that shape and configure an improvisational space.

Motion Through Space. One can liken the process of filling a space with movement to making brush strokes on a canvas. Jumps make little dots or discrete quick brush strokes, while floor work or traveling leaps make long flowing lines. Using all of the available space communicates something. Choosing to not use all of the space says something else. People see space, even when it's not being used (i.e., negative space on a canvas is the area that is in between the boundaries of objects). Places through which you move, and places where you stop to rest, can be considered as a kinesthetic spatial design.

Descriptive Variables for Moving in Space

Terms that help us describe and know more about the way we use space include pattern, shape, and juxtaposition.

Pattern refers to the path we trace on the floor. Movements can flow continuously or they can jump from one discrete action to the next. Patterns are also constant or repetitive postures, actions, thoughts, and emotions. They can prevent us from meeting our needs in the most efficient, effective, and enjoyable way. Over the years, we become so used to set ways of moving, thinking, feeling, and acting that they become habits or patterns. As a result, these habitual ways of behaving unconsciously control parts of us. Our physical health, relationships, work performance, eating habits, and posture can all be affected. Unpatterning is the process of unlearning patterns and rediscovering alternatives. It dissolves blocks and restores the flow of matter and energy to the most efficient paths. Unpatterning involves a conscious decision to reroute the paths we are most drawn to take.

Shape refers to the shape of the body when taking individual movements (e.g., is the body elongated or is it squashed and flat) and to the shape of the movements placed against themselves (e.g., are they rounded or held at angles to one another).

Juxtaposition refers to how the group of individuals makes a shape in space. Juxtaposition deals with how you are placed in relation to other people and objects that share your space.

Body Work – Space

1. *Increasing awareness and facility with space.* This activity is a good one for learning about the limits of the 'canvas' or stage upon which you paint your motions.
   a) In fifteen seconds (time it with a stop watch or have someone else time it) cover as much space as possible.
   b) In the next fifteen seconds, ask a second person to try to cover even more space. The second person will attempt to use spaces neglected by the first (e.g., up high, down low, in the corners).
   c) Repeat this with a third, fourth, or fifth person, as many as are willing to try. What new spaces were covered by subsequent participants? Did these new spaces broaden your notions about available space?

2. *Shape.* Strike a pose and notice the shape of your body in this pose. Experiment with several different poses and see how your body feels in each of these designs. Look at yourself in the mirror as you pose. What sort of visual statements do the shapes make?

3. *Juxtaposition.* You need a mirror and a group of people (at least 3) to try this exercise. Have one person in the group strike a pose. Then add the second person's pose, which must relate to the first pose in some way. Add the others in this same way. Pause in between each additional person to watch (in a mirror, if you can) the many different shapes that the group can form.

4. *Patterns.* Work out a floor pattern that involves four different motions. Choose a partner, and teach your floor pattern to your partner. Have your partner teach you the pattern that (s)he has created. How does it feel to move through space with this new pattern? How does it increase your options for movement?

Combine the two floor patterns into an eight step dance. Demonstrate the new pattern you have created together. How is it the same or different from moving in your old predictable way? How does this new pattern feel different or the same as your partner's four step dance?

5. Take the patterns you created in the previous exercise and diagram them on a piece of paper or a chalkboard. What kind of design do your movements make when they are transcribed in this way? Look at the visual patterns and ask yourself again the questions posed in exercise 2. What new insights arise when you view your creation in this visual way?

6. *Letting Go.* Allowing your body to experience the sensation of falling is a kinesthetic way of breaking down patterns, of letting go.

Experiment with different ways of falling – let different parts of the body fall, fall in different directions, fall at different rates. Do not force yourself to do something you are afraid of, but see how you can accomplish your goal of falling and letting go.

Continue as above, but let the momentum of your falling body carry you up into a new movement. Write down (or discuss) how the new movements feel.

*   *   *   *   *

This completes our conceptual and kinesthetic investigations into how the body moves in time and space. We have sensed Time and Space alternately as finite resources and as potentialities, as limitations and as boundaries for our creative flow. This duality holds true for another facet of our physical lives – namely, the aspect of weight. The fact that bodies have mass and substance influences our movements and our entire physical lives in a prominent way. Therefore, the next topic of investigation is the subject of **weight**.

Chapter 6

WEIGHT

Every adult needs a rock, a ground for his identity.
– Erik Ericson

What is Weight?

When I ask myself that question, I find that I don't have a clear cut, simple answer. I know that I am supposed to measure something called weight when I jump on the bathroom scale. I have learned from junior high science class that weight is the result of gravity pulling upon the mass of a body. If I travel to the top of a tall mountain, somehow I don't seem to have as much weight, and if I were an astronaut traveling through outer space, my attraction to the earth, or my weight, would be almost nil. When I eat a lot of food at a holiday meal, it is very probable that I will weigh more. Is there truly a quality of weight, or is it merely a quantity, a number on a scale? Weight seems to be more a characteristic of the environment than a trait that describes me, myself.

In the quantitative aspect of weight, the human body differs little from other aggregations of matter, even the inorganic. As is true for all objects with mass, the gravitational pull of the earth is a potent physical influence on human life. On earth, gravity is with us from the time of our conception to the moment of our death. It is so all pervading that we cannot sense it, for humans perceive sensory stimulation only as it varies (e.g., we recognize light after periods of darkness and sound because we know quiet). We do not directly sense gravity or weight, but we recognize their effects.

In human bodies, gravity acts to shorten, thicken and compress. Bodies are designed to contact the earth. We stand on our feet, and the primary human posture fights against the pull of gravity to rise up erect and tall. Individual body units (e.g., head, thorax, pelvis, legs) are heavy enough to have significant gravitational existence on their own. A set of toy building blocks offers an interesting analogy. Any child knows that if (s)he stacks the blocks vertically with the center of gravity of each block being vertically above the center of gravity of its neighbor below, (s)he will create a stable structure. Similarly, our bodies work best when the centers of gravity of the aggregate parts are built upon one another, rather than scattered in all directions. A slight shift from our natural alignment (e.g., head or neck forward, distended abdomen, or swayback) lets gravity seize the displaced area. Without a streamlined bone-through-bone flow to distribute our weight, we are slowly and steadily pulled down. (See Chapter 3 on **posture** for more on the subject of gravity's effects on human structure.)

Linguistic Associations

I find it fascinating that the words 'gravity', 'weight', 'substance', and 'seriousness' are all synonyms. Serious, significant matters are described as 'weighty'. These kinds of issues have 'substance', in other words they are important. Such situations have a great deal of 'gravity'. When the weight of a situation becomes too great, it becomes a 'burden' or 'too much to handle'. Relative to this, the contrary quality – lightness – is perceived as a blessing or relief from the burden of a heavy weight.

When I 'throw my weight' into a project, I am talking about putting my whole self into the task. When an idea 'carries weight', it is likely to be considered important and to have an inherent power to change events. A 'heavy' problem is likely to be one with many consequences and far-reaching effects. What is true for the physical world also holds true for counterparts in the psychological realm. We cannot explain the gravity or weight of a psychological condition, but we recognize its many effects. Just as with the physical phenomenon of gravity or weight, we envision a powerful force acting at a distance, but cannot elaborate on how or why the action occurs.

This text will examine some essential characteristics of weight, rather than regarding weight as an entity in itself. The physical effects of weight and mass can teach us many Bodylessons. Among these are lessons about **balance** and equilibrium, **centering** and grounding, and **resistance** or lessons about leaning on and being leaned on by others. These three essential properties will be discussed in turn.

Therefore the format of this chapter will vary slightly from other chapter formats. First, a warm-up designed to introduce the experience of weight is presented. Then, each essential property (**balance, centering,** and **resistance**) will be conceptually discussed and laid out separately with its own accompanying Body Work. This layout will, I hope, allow for a clearer presentation than mixing all the concepts together indiscriminately.

A Warm-up Exercise

You need three people to carry out this investigation. One will pretend to be a balloon. The other two will bat and push the balloon around. That is all there is to it. Continue playing for about five minutes, then change roles. Keep repeating the activity until everyone gets a chance to be the balloon. What has this simple demonstration taught you about lightness, heaviness, and weight?

BALANCE

Balance is more than just achieving a stable point that will not tip over. Balancing requires us to continually consider the dynamic mix of events of our lives and to discover 'just how much is the right amount' in relation to each. When our lives are in balance, everything that we do (e.g., work, play, family, etc.) fits in and complements every other part of our lives. When any one component is out of kilter (e.g., you are putting in a lot of unwanted overtime at work), the quality of the whole life experience is diminished.

Homeostasis

Analogously, the human body depends upon a delicate balance to maintain itself. Physiological homeostasis involves an active regulation of acceptable amounts of heat and cold, activity and rest, and numerous other settings.

Let us examine the way our bodies maintain the fine balance between heat and cold. Our bodies simply cannot function if they get too hot. Above 105 degrees F, the proteins that make up much of the human body literally fry like an egg. Proteins are the main stuffs of enzymes, for instance. Enzymes are the catalysts for the body's chemical reactions. Thus, the chemical reactions that ordinarily keep the body moving come to a standstill if the human body reaches a temperature above 105 degrees F. Nor can we work optimally when we get too cold. Many vital metabolic reactions, such as the digestion of food, must take place at a certain minimal temperature or they will not occur at all. The body also goes haywire and stops functioning when it goes outside of certain blood sugar, ph balance, and water solubility limits.

When you begin to pay attention to the way you move, you immediately recognize the need for balance. Not only professional athletes, but also amateur weekend-only players continually strive for balance in their sport of choice. Football, tennis and golf players alike all try to control their movements so that they are neither too slow nor too fast, too weak or too strong, and not leaning too far to the side.

Body Work – Balance

1. *Hatha Yoga Asanas to Improve Balance.* Not only will regular practice of balancing poses lead to improved balance, but it will also prove to be an invaluable aid to greater concentration and focus.

   a) Tree Pose (Vrikasan) to begin, stand with your feet together. Steady yourself by fixing your gaze on a spot on the wall in front of you. (You can hold on to the back of a chair to brace yourself, at first.) Place your right foot against the inside of your left leg, with the toes pointed toward the floor. (If your foot will not go high enough to rest on your thigh, brace it against your knee.) Because of the concentration required to maintain balance, you may find that you have a tendency to hold your breath. Keep breathing. When you feel steady and comfortable balancing on one leg, slowly bring your arms up overhead and place the palms together. Hold the asana for about ten seconds. Repeat once on each side.

b) Dancer Pose (Natarajasan) (Caution: those with lower back and disc problems should not do this exercise without medical supervision.) Fix your gaze on one spot for balance. Grasp your left foot with your right hand. Raise your left arm overhead, pointed toward the ceiling, next to your ear. Slowly and carefully lift your left leg up and away from your body. Hold the pose, continuing to breathe easily for several seconds. Relax and repeat on the opposite side.

2. *Exploring Physical/Emotional Balance.* Right now, take a moment to stand up and balance on one leg. If it is easy for you to balance, do so with your eyes closed. Make a mental note of how easy or difficult it is for you to do. The next time you are 'upset', either with anger, sadness, or another emotion, see if you can disengage yourself enough to explore the effect of the upset emotions on your body. You can do this by re-administering the above-mentioned balance test. If you continue to think about how upset you are it will be relatively difficult to balance. On the other hand, if you concentrate on balancing, you may find yourself feeling less upset. Physical and emotional balance go hand in hand. Emphasis on one exerts an influence on the other.

3. *Overcompensation.* Synthesized from several methods advocated by Dan Millman in *The Warrior Athlete*, this exercise is especially designed for people who want to correct an unbalanced way of moving. For example, if you pull the ball to the left when you play softball, then on your next attempt, purposely hit too far to the right. The next time you play, dedicate a certain portion of your attention and effort to consciously maintaining this off-balance position. By purposely doing something way out of balance, you can observe the action more clearly. Although this will feel extremely awkward, it will help you see your actions from a

new perspective. When you go back to moving in the old way, it will not feel the same. Use this unsettled feeling to help you find a more appropriate balance of forces for you.

CENTERING

When we say that we are 'centered', we mean that we have found our center of balance and we feel right at home where we are. When your energy is centered you need less muscle power to work and move. Actions are more powerful when they radiate from a strong center. With a strong source, energy can flow freely out through the arms and the hands. Being centered entails finding the correct posture and remaining 'grounded' or aware of your contact with the ground through your legs and feet. This is like a tree whose roots go down deep into the earth. When we seek the center, we seek our inner-most core, the heart of the matter, so to speak. A center is always found within oneself.

The Physical Center of the Human Body – The Hara

Hara is the Japanese word for belly or abdomen, the soft area between the rib cage and the pelvic bone. In Oriental medicine, the central source for vital energy and strength is considered to live here in a point a few inches below the navel. Most of the organs of the body are situated in and around the hara. All of the body's vital metabolic functions are active here. Geographically, the belly is located in the most central zone of our bodies. Considering all these facts, it is easy to see how the hara can act as a center of gravity, power, equilibrium, and stability. When you work from the hara, you can operate with power but without effort or strain.

The vital spirit is also said to reside in the hara. In Japan, 'hara' describes the quality of one's energy. You may have a good or bad hara and to kill yourself is to kill the hara (hara-kiri).

Psychological Centering

From a psychological standpoint, centering is a process of finding the source of strength, clarity, and peace within. It is a way of focusing, of gathering your energy into a point so that you can channel it more easily into any activity you choose. Centering creates higher levels of awareness and enhances your ability to discover what is most important and meaningful to you. When you are centered, you feel calm, quiet, strong, secure, balanced, present in the moment and able to deal with pressures surrounding you.

Many disciplines recommend finding an imaginary mental center for the attention. An inner center is a safe haven inside yourself where you can 'go' anytime or anywhere. It is a place of special power where you can drop all tensions and demands of the outside world. Your center or sanctuary is an ideal place for relaxation, tranquility, and safety, and you can create or recreate it any way that you want.

Body Work – Centering

1. *Exercise to center the body.* With eyes closed, gently rock from side to side, from one foot to the other. Use this pendulum motion to help find just the right point of balance for your body. Allow the head to rock until it finds a balance, too. Gradually slow the motion until the body is still, feeling the balance of the head on top of the cervical vertebrae. Concentrate on the pelvis acting as an anchor for the body, with the legs grounding the body to the earth, and the spine resting on top of the pelvis. Feel the spine in alignment, and the head resting on top of the spine. Focus on the shoulder blades and feel them like a crossbar, balanced off of the spine. There is no need to hold the shoulders; they are balanced from the spine, and the arms fall in relaxation from the shoulders. How does it feel to find your center in this way?

2. *Exercise to center your mind.* This is adapted from *Creating a Sanctuary,* by Shakti Gawain. Close your eyes and relax in a comfortable position. Imagine yourself in some beautiful natural environment. Think of any

place that appeals to you . . . a meadow, mountaintop, forest, or ocean. It could even be under the sea or on another planet. Wherever you go, it should feel comfortable, peaceful, and pleasant. Explore the environment, noticing sights, sounds, smells, and tastes, along with any other impressions. Do whatever you like to make the place more homelike and comfortable. You might want to surround the area with a bubble of safety, rearrange the setting for more convenience, or perform a ritual to establish this as your special place. You can come to this center anytime that you like. All you need do is close your eyes and imagine it. You may want to change your center from time to time, or you may find that it seems to spontaneously evolve on its own.

RESISTANCE

Physical Resistance

As we hold an object high above the ground, we can physically feel the resistance of its weight. We feel pressure, heaviness, and a focus for our efforts. Similar sensations arise in response to the weight of someone else's body as it pushes or pulls against our own. We can observe how the weight of a human body causes it to fall to the ground. Weight lifting is an example of how we can harness resistance in a beneficial way. By focusing on the resistance of weights and working against their mass, we gradually build muscle and develop our bodies. The exercises at the end of this section ask you to pay attention to how your body, mind, and emotions respond when you are working against a physical mass. As you complete your experiments, make sure to write down observations. This kinesthetic information can translate into useful strategies for knocking down nonphysical barriers (e.g., emotions, attitudes) as well as physical ones.

Psychological Resistance

If you think of the hardest thing for you to do and how much you resist it, then you're looking at your greatest lesson at the moment. Psychological resistance can appear on many levels and it can become apparent in the form of non-verbal clues, delaying tactics, excuses, denial and fear.

Often, our actions show resistance when we deny it with words. Non-verbal clues that let us know we are fighting against internal demons include changing the subject, leaving the room, being late, getting sick, doing busy work, wasting time, looking away, flipping through a book, not paying attention, or eating, drinking or smoking too much.

Delaying tactics sound like this: "I'll do it later, I don't have the time, I have too much else to do, it's too late, it's too soon, the time isn't right." We can also deny that a problem exists with phrases like, "Nothing is wrong", "If I ignore it, maybe the problem will go away", or "There is nothing I can do."

Fear of changing crops up in the following excuses, "I'm not ready", "I might fail", "I might get hurt", "It's too hard", "I'm not good enough" or "I don't know enough", "It might cost me money", and "I might lose something."

Other excuses place the power for fixing the situation outside of one-self, on a mysterious 'them.' 'They' won't approve, it's all 'their' fault, 'they' won't understand, 'they' won't allow it; I don't want to hurt 'them'.

Resistance is supported by a number of beliefs, assumptions and self-concepts that can be identified and changed.

Some limiting beliefs are, "I'm not that kind of person", "It's not right", "It's too expensive", or "It takes too long."

We have so many false self-concepts that it would be impossible to list them all. Generally, a false self-concept can be recognized by its preface, "I'm too . . .". You can fill in the blank with the adjective of choice (e.g., old, fat, young, thin, short, tall, weak, lazy, dumb, smart, poor). Almost any descriptor would work. All are notions about ourselves that serve as barriers to change.

Underlying attitudes or assumptions also help to justify resistance.

Some of these are "Only crazy people do that", "My case is special or different", and "Nobody else would do that."

Body Work – Resistance

1. *Exploring the resistance of objects.* Locate two objects of different weights (e.g. an apple and a feather). Pick up one of the objects and put it down, then pick up the other object and put it down, sensing the difference between the two. Is it easy to sense the difference in weight?

This time pick up one of the objects again, but before you do, tense your arm, shoulder, wrist, and fingers as tightly as you can. Grasp each object tightly before lifting. Lift one object, then the other, as you tense. Did you notice that it was more difficult to feel a weight difference?

2. *Manikins/Rag dolls.* In this exploration, one person becomes like a 'rag doll' and the other gets to play with it. To begin, the rag doll lets go of all tension in the body, and becomes like a dead weight. The mover can place the rag doll's limbs, torso, and head in any position (s)he chooses. The rag doll moves easily into position, but once a position is decided upon, the rag doll remains in that pose until moved. Explore the effect of weight upon the rag doll using this method. Then reverse roles and do the exercise again.

3. *Mirroring resistance.* Physical contact between two people can teach much about resistance. Contact mirroring involves mirroring PLUS an exchange of weight. (See the mirroring exercises in Chapter 12 on **reaction** vs. **response**.) This improvisational technique involves actual touching, as opposed to simple gesture. As the leader presses in, so does the follower. When the initiator leans out, the imitator does the same. This way, the leader immediately feels the weight of his/her actions. To begin, select a partner and without speaking or using any signs, mutually decide who will first initiate the action. The leader performs movements and the follower mirrors them, without any lapse in time. After five minutes, change roles. What did you observe about the effect of your resistance? What effect did resistance have on you?

4. A cantilever is defined as: a member projecting beyond a fulcrum and supported by a balancing member (or downward force) behind the fulcrum. In this activity, two partners extend their weight out to fuse and structurally intermingle (e.g., one could reach out with an arm and the other could rest her leg on the extended arm). Instead of two separate objects with two distinct centers of mass they join to form a new mass with a shared center of weight between. The point of this exploration is to find out how the new mass behaves. Where did a center establish itself? How do the forces depend on each other to sustain a joint posture? This weight dependency exercise offers a shared experience of movement, a shared use of two bodies. How does it feel to literally 'lift', 'pull', 'lean on one another', and 'push to the limits'?

*   *   *   *   *

According to quantum physics (symbolized by Einstein's $E=mc^2$), matter and energy are two sides of the same coin. Although this concept may be somewhat difficult to fathom, we can intuitively sense that human beings literally embody both matter and energy. There is something like a 'life energy' that comes together with matter to produce the miracle of a living being. This next Bodylesson, **energy**, is an exploration of the spirit that brings our physical body mass to life.

Chapter 7

ENERGY

Every part of us that is sensitive and alive is spirit;
and everything in us, from head to toe, is alive
and sensitive.
– Emanuel Swedenborg

When we think of energy, we tend to think of some kind of natural physical force – such as heat, light, mechanical energy (e.g., moving water or blowing air), chemical reactions (e.g., the power behind our battery cells), or electricity. The pounding of an ocean's surf is one kind of natural energy that is always present when the ocean meets the shore; it is waves of energy in action. Natural energy waves are also a part of the human body. The heart, for example, is beating pulsations of blood all throughout the body. The heartbeat is a slow vibration of working energy. As you breathe air in and out of the lungs, you create and use another type of slow pulsating energy wave. Talking creates faster waves of vibrational energy in the air. When you listen, the ear transforms one vibrational energy into another that the brain can understand. All of these movements are natural energy vibrations that the human body generates and uses in every moment. Waves of energy are a part of you – your own life energy belonging to you and no one else.

Life Energy

Prana

According to Indian tradition, the word for life-energy is 'prana'. Swami Sri Satchidananda calls prana the vital link between body and mind, because without it we cannot continue to live.

Pranayama (breathing exercises) demonstrate the integral connection between energy and breath. As was previously mentioned, prana literally means 'life force' or 'life energy', and yama can roughly be translated as 'control'. Thus pranayama refers to the voluntary manipulation of the life force, and is an integral part of yoga. Breath is the vehicle for prana. Our language indicates an intuitive recognition of the relationship between breath and energy, and the necessity of energy for life. When someone dies, and the energy and vitality have gone, we say that (s)he has 'expired', that the breath has 'gone out', the energy has left. The body remains but life force dissipates. When someone shows increased mental energy and creativity, we say that (s)he has become 'inspired', that there is an 'inspiration'.

Respiration may very well be the only physiological process that can be under voluntary or involuntary control. One can alter the breath by speeding it up or slowing it down or by making it more or less regular. Or one can give up conscious control and allow their breathing to become a reflex action. When the breath is ignored, the body simply takes in air on its own. The body cannot function without oxygen. When conscious command of respiration is abandoned, some unconscious part of the mind begins functioning and breathes for us. Some basic instinct in the limbic system stimulates breathing. When we allow non-conscious respiration – which is controlled by these primitive brain structures – thoughts and feelings tend to interfere with the regulation of functions. Taking in life energy becomes haphazard and often irregular when we give up, forget, or ignore conscious mastery of the breath.

Breathing influences both body and mind. The rhythm and rate of your breathing not only reflect the body's physical condition, but also help create it. Notice how breathing is an excellent indicator of emotional and mental states. When you are worried or excited, your respiration rate increases and the breath becomes shallow. When you are calm and centered, breathing slows down and becomes more regular.

Voluntary manipulation of the breath (pranayama) can influence and help create desirable emotional and mental states. Do you remember your parent's advice to count to ten before you get into a fight? When you count to ten, you are giving your body an opportunity to take ten deep breaths. Those ten deep breaths help relax and free you to see other options. Smoking cessation programs use this concept to alleviate the compulsion to smoke. Counting to ten gives the deep breathing a chance to relax the body on its own. It allows enough time to elapse for you to realize that you can calm down even without a cigarette. Thus, taking an active role in observing and influencing a metabolic function like breathing can have some very real consequences for our physical and psychic states.

Ki/Chi

In karate, breath control is known as ki (internal energy) control, and it involves centralization and extension. Centralization means focusing on the belly (hara) to establish a foundation of strength and stability. Extension involves three features. First, ki extends around the body like a magnetic field. This is to sense and ward off danger before it touches the physical body. From there, ki spreads into a weapon (e.g., a fist, foot, stick, or sword) and projects out the eye in order to frighten the challenger. Eye ki allows one to see clearly with 'eyes of God' that spot unseen danger and know an opponent's true motivations. Finally, ki merges with the energy of the attacker, allowing the stronger power to triumph.

The word 'ki' is actually used in several ways in aikido, and in Eastern thought generally. Aikido is literally translated as the way (Do) of harmony (Ai) with the spirit of the universe (Ki). Aikido is a Japanese art of self-defense, inspired by Morehei Uyeshiba, where the spirit is of working with your partner, not of fighting an opponent. In the broadest sense, ki is spirit or energy, the flow of love and life energy, the manifestation of harmony. Ki (or chi as the Chinese call it) exists in many forms, from the purest, such as light, to the most coarse, such as the energy that has been captured in volcanic rock. When we break apart matter (fission) we get an explosion of energy.

Ki can be either deficient or in excess, and sometimes it can be blocked. You may have experienced having too much or too little energy, or not being able to access it when you want. When you have too little energy you feel tired, listless and run down. When you have too much, you are likely to feel excitable, unable to relax, perhaps angry and impatient. When your energy is blocked, a feeling of frustration is liable to occur.

Other Terms for Life Force

In addition to prana and ki, there are many other words that are used to talk about life energy. In Japan, for instance, 'hara' expresses the quality of one's energy. Likewise, the 'chi' in Tai Chi Chuan (Supreme Ultimate Martial Art Way) is energy. It is the same energy that can be experienced when we are frightened or angry. At those times our energy level for 'fight or flight' arises. The same rising of energy occurs in anger, haste, or any strong emotional reaction. This sensation is due to the physical process of adrenaline being released into our bloodstream.

Wilhelm Reich used the term 'orgone' and Leibnitz hypothesized the existence of 'monads' to describe the spirit that gives vitality to a corporeal being. Chi, ki, prana, hara, orgone, monads, the élan vital – all refer to the life spirit within us, our vitality, our spark, our life essence.

E (energy) in Motion = Emotions

I believe that emotions actually derive from the movement of finer points of energy. Carl Jung pointed out that the concept of energy actually derives from a psychological feeling of being energetic. Isn't it curious that we use the same word, 'feelings', to represent both physical and emotional sensation? William James first promulgated the notion that emotion has a physical basis. He asked a question that is still relevant today, "Does the emotional excitement which follows (an) idea follow it immediately, or secondarily and as a consequence of the 'diffusive wave' of (physical) impulses aroused?" That is, are the physical sensations that accompany our emotions a secondary manifestation, or do the physiological changes come first? James hypothesized that there must be a process of some sort in the nerve centers for emotion, and he further hypothesized that the process involved affective 'currents' of energy.

James proposed an experiment to test his theory. He said that if emotions are a consequence of movement, then a person who was completely anesthetized should not be able to feel happy or sad or angry or anything. A colleague of James', Sollier, carried out just such an experiment. When complete peripheral and visceral anesthesia were given to a female patient, she 'felt no normal emotion whatsoever'. When anesthesia was less complete, she reported physical sensations rather than emotions. And when only peripheral anesthesia was administered, almost normal emotional responses were observed. Albert Ax further illuminated the physical responses that accompany emotion by studying forty-three patients' physiological reactions to fear and anger-provoking stimuli. He found that recorded physiological reaction patterns were clearly different for the two stimuli. Decrease in heart rate, increase in diastolic blood pressure and integrated muscle potential, and number of increases in skin conductance were greater for anger; whereas increase in skin conductance and respiration rate along with number of increases in muscle potential were greater for fear.

Sexual Energy

One of the most powerful forms of bodily energy that animals possess is sexual potency. When the human animal is attracted to someone, the body creates changes that can be physically felt. Some of us tend to lose our appetite, for example, and feel a sense of excitement that we cannot explain.

This is a physiological manifestation of a change in energy. Physical attraction is sometimes described in terms of a magnet metaphor. We find ourselves being emotionally and physically 'pulled' towards the one that we desire. In a similar way, there is an energy inside of us that naturally draws us towards activities and experiences that we wish to partake in. This excitement, this attraction, this energy can be drawn upon to improve our performance in any situation we choose. For decades, athletes and salesmen have been harnessing this 'spark of inspiration'. Now all of us can do the same.

The Spark of Inspiration, Excitement and Energy

When you become quiet inside and listen for the sound of your own breath, you may begin to notice a natural pause before each inhalation. And if you can get very quiet within, you may notice a little spark of energy at the end of each pause. That is the spark that provides the impetus for the next inbreath. Because your body wants air, it creates an impulse to inhale. A burst of energy from within leads our bodies effortlessly to the desired goal – a new breath. Air seems to come in almost by itself. There is nothing that you have to do. In this case, you have experienced the spark of inspiration. It comes from the same deep level and the same sense of natural ease that energy and inspiration come from when you are performing at your highest level.

Optimal Use of Energy

Perhaps you can recall an event in your past in which you performed optimally. An optimal performance would be an event that was a real 'high', a time when you were very successful, or maybe a moment when you achieved true excellence. Recreating this special event in your mind can help you remember qualities that allowed you to succeed. Remembering how that spark of inspiration felt allows it to become more accessible and to support you in other strivings.

Perhaps you can even step back into that scene. You may remember your purpose in preparing for that event. What was your goal? What was in it for you? How much did you care about it? Can you sense the tension within, the desire, the energy that stimulated you to strive for excellence? You do not need words to describe the feeling. What is important is to feel the sensation. Where do you sense the energy in your body? If you can relive the event from beginning to end, other impressions will begin to emerge. You can actually feel the excitement as you feel the excellence in your body. You may notice your breath getting deeper and fuller, and you may recognize the familiar spark of inspiration. Right at the moment where you actualize your goal, you may feel a surge of power, a boundless internal strength, and an eagerness to move. This is **energy** that you have harnessed in the past. Be aware that this is power that you can call upon again to meet challenges that arise in the future.

Body Work

1. *Energy and breath – manipulating energy levels.* Concentrate on the inbreath, as you breathe slowly and fully through the nose. To enhance the effect of this practice, say to yourself the word, 'energy', as you take in the breath. What you may notice is an increase in energy level and vitality that accompanies attention on the inbreath.

Now, try concentrating on the outbreath as you are breathing out slowly and fully through the nostrils. To enhance this effect, say the word, 'relax', with every exhalation. Notice what happens to your energy level when you change the emphasis to the outbreath.

2. *Feeling your energy ball.* Hold your hands in front of you as if you were holding a ball. Now play with that imaginary sphere, molding it, feeling it grow or shrink in size. Can you feel vibrations emanating from your hands as if they held a ball of energy? These vibrations are emanating from your hands all of the time, only you usually are not attuned to them. For the rest of the day, try to notice any sensations originating from your palms, fingers, or backs of the hands.

3. *Sharing energy.* Once you experience your ball of energy, you can go about sharing it with someone else. If you have found that you can easily create the energy ball, continue to mold and play with your creation.

Ask a partner to create a ball for him/herself. Now see if the two of you can combine your energy balls into one energy sphere. How does the combined sphere feel to each of you? Is this creation more powerful than the energy ball you made on your own? Is it the same size?

4. *How much is enough energy?* This easy hatha yoga warm-up helps you to gauge just how much energy is enough for you. You find the balance between too little and too much energy. To begin, stand with your arms at the side and exhale. Now start to inhale, bringing out the arms slightly and rising up on tiptoe. Fix your gaze on a spot on the wall in front of you to help balance. (Do not look down at the floor, because your body will follow that focus and you will topple over.) Complete the inhalation, and as you are rising make gentle fists and bring them up under your rib cage to help support the lifting motion. Hold the balance and the breath for a short while – long enough to experience the 'spark of inspiration'. Then exhale as you come down on your heels and relax the arms at your side. Notice your energy level as you rise. If you bring too much force and energy to the lifting, you will topple over. If the energy that you manage to muster is too little for the task, you will not be able to rise at all.

5. *What do you do with excess energy?* For this inquiry, all you need do is observe how you respond in times when you are experiencing lots of energy. You are most likely to catch yourself in a high energy state during moments of excitement (e.g., when your team has won the big game or after you have just received a promotion at work). When you are filled with a lot of energy you may become aware of the coursing of your blood and the pumping of your heart. The object of this lesson is to make a mental note to watch and see where all of that energy goes. What happens after the initial burst of energy? Where does it go? Most of us do not have a strategy for making use of a 'rush' of energy. We do not know how to save our power for future times when we may be feeling lackluster and dull. All too often, we waste the accumulated energy by picking a fight or getting angry over a matter of little consequence, or maybe by just feeling unsettled and uneasy. Wouldn't it be great if, instead

of wasting our energy, we could harness the excess for constructive purposes? Right now, take some time to do just that. Make a list of things that you like to do when you have so much energy that you don't know what to do with yourself (e.g., exercising to burn off steam, or polishing off some normally unpleasant but physical chore, like vacuuming).

*   *   *   *   *

When we begin to sense the energy that is always present within our bodies, it is almost as if we have to find a way of expressing what we feel. Movement can be a magical tool for transforming and sharing our energies with the world. The internal machinations that transpire inside our corporeal shells long to be set free – to be expressed. Moving our physical bodies can allow us to truly be ourselves and to reveal energies that would otherwise remain locked within. In the next chapter, we will concentrate on the value of movement as an **expression** of our bodies.

Chapter 8

EXPRESSION

If a seed is given good soil and plenty of water and sun,
it doesn't have to try to unfold. It doesn't need self-con-
fidence or self-discipline or perseverance. It just unfolds.
As a matter of fact, it can't help unfolding.
– Molly Groger

Express yourself.
– Salt-N'-Pepa

Everything that we do throughout the course of our lives is an expression of our being. Each day we express new thoughts and feelings about the colors, events, places, and things that enter into our experience. We express ourselves in a myriad of actions. We do so in the way we dress, the products we buy, the places we visit and the way that we move.

All of the arts – poetry and prose, drawing and painting, song and movement – help us to express ourselves in a more profound way. In this chapter, we will examine how movement can express some of our deepest thoughts and feelings and how body expression can clue us into what we really are.

The Human Body is an Expressive Instrument

The body truly is like another entity with its own perspective, its own slant, its own unique view. A person may be voicing one opinion while the body indicates an entirely different view. In fact, the use of lie detectors is based on just such a premise. Lie detectors measure changes in physiological activity such as galvanic skin response (the amount of mois ture on the skin), heart rate, breathing rate, and muscle tension. It is presumed that when someone tells a lie, these sorts of physiological functions fluctuate. A less 'scientific' kinesiology test can illustrate the body's ability to act as a lie detector. This simple test involves no equipment at all, just you and a partner. All you need do is extend your arm out to the side, and have a companion try to push the arm down. Do it once to establish a baseline for comparison. How much effort is needed to resist the push? Now say several statements aloud, some true (e.g., "I enjoy going out to dine"), some false (e.g., "I want to work overtime"), and each time repeat the arm test as you verbalize the statement. Notice the relative strength of your arm as your friend pushes down with a constant force. Many people see a correspondence between the veracity of the statement and the strength of their arm . . . almost as if the limb becomes a truth gauge. Try it for yourself.

Body Language

The demonstration outlined above illustrates in a crude way how bodies can reveal much about what we really think and feel. In fact, a new field of study has arisen to detail the effects of body language. Over 60% of the messages sent in a conversation are non-verbal body language. Elements that can help or hinder our communications include proxemics and kinesics messages.

Proxemics comes from the same base as proximity – how near or far you are to other people. A convenient way to think of proxemics is as personal space, referring to the amount of space required between you and others in order to feel comfortable. It is believed that the need to establish a territory is a throwback to our survival instinct. To invade one's personal space is threatening and to take more than your share (e.g., by throwing a coat over the seat in front of you) is an aggressive act. Social psychologists have determined that Americans, on average, need about a two- to three-foot elliptical bubble of space between themselves and others in order to feel secure. The ellipse is narrower along the sides and wider in front and in back. For effective conversation, you need more space . . . four to six feet is an optimal distance. When others intrude on an individual's imaginary bubble (unless they are invited in for a hug or some other physical intimacy), the individual will alleviate tension by stepping back or turning to one side. The same person needs less space when (s)he is feeling healthy and expansive and more space when (s)he is feeling vulnerable. Have you ever watched a person who has just been insulted? It is not uncommon to see them backing away from the one who initiated the verbal attack.

The size of the ellipse also tends to vary by culture and ethnicity. Manners that you have grown up with and become accustomed to will affect your sense of personal space. In general (and this does not hold true for all individuals in a given culture), people from warm climates such as Latin America like to get close to one another when they talk. Their personal ellipse is relatively small. Conversely, people from northern cultures such as Germanic or British people need more space to be comfortable; their personal ellipse is relatively large. You could conceivably find two people with different personal comfort zones holding a conversation on the move. One is constantly moving forward, continually trying to get closer, while the other is furiously trying to ease the tension by backing away.

Kinesics refers to the movement and gestures that we make with or without words. Kinesics is, in effect, a second language. It is a sequence of subtle, ubiquitous behaviors that accompany everything we say and do, and are extremely difficult to observe. You may be familiar with some of the more common gestures: inclining the head forward tends to indicate receptivity while leaning it back shows apathy and indifference; skin stroking is often an evaluative-type motion, the kind of motion you might associate with a professor considering whether to change a grade; playing with an object, such as tapping a pencil, can indicate distraction, that an individual is not really paying attention. So, if you came to me with a problem, and I stroked my chin, leaned forward, and turned to look you straight in the eye, you might reasonably think that I was interested in what you had to say. On the other hand, if I leaned back in the chair, played with a little rubber ball, and only glanced up occasionally over my glasses, you might deduce that I was unsympathetic, even apathetic.

towards your cause. My actions would be saying that, "After all, it wasn't even worth my while to focus."

Every part of the human figure can be an expressive speaker. The head, for instance, houses most of the sense organs and reacts very quickly to stimuli. Just as it is human nature to shield the eyes from strong sunlight, closing the eyes helps to shut out people who are sending unwanted signals. Because the neck is a crucial area for survival, messages involving that area can be very telling. When we feel threatened, we instinctively act to protect the neck (e.g., by shrugging or reaching under the collar). Thousands of nerve endings make the hands and fingers one of the body's most sensitive and expressive zones. Exposed palms open us up to stimuli sent by others, and show that we are in a more accepting mood. The chest or trunk is important because it is the area most responsible for posture. As discussed in Chapter 3, posture is a clear indicator of our attitudes. The pelvis is the great taboo zone of the body. Many feelings and urges develop here. And the legs and feet may be the most irrepressible speakers of all. These extremities are about as far away as you can get from the head and the logic and reserve of the intellect. Leg and feet signals can be quite blatant (e.g., impatient tapping or uncomfortable crossing and uncrossing of the legs).

Please be cautioned that there is a vast complexity to kinesics. Interpretations are best deciphered slowly, over time, through continued observation and experience. What our bodies seem to be saying is not always what they are trying to convey.

The Face

Faces can reveal a great deal about true inner feelings, or they can serve as a false front to mask what we wish to keep hidden. People say, "Don't look so sad", or, "Put on a happy face." The kind of face we put on can alternately reveal or hide much about who we are, what we want, and how we feel. In our language, we speak of 'facing the world', 'presenting a face', or creating a 'facade'.

Smiling, sad, and angry faces are all easily recognizable, even to observers from a totally foreign culture. Paul Ekman maintains that universal facial expressions are shared by all people and understood without translation among different cultures. Expressions of fear, anger, or disgust cause the same physiological changes in people from widely different cultures. When Indonesians make certain facial gestures, they experience identical changes in skin temperature, heart rate, and perspiration output as Americans making the same faces. "What binds us as humans," says Ekman, professor of psychology at the University of California at San Francisco and principal investigator for these studies, "is that we have the same expressions for emotions and the same feelings to accompany . . . emotions." Ekman and his colleagues also asked tribal volunteers in western Sumatra to show fear, anger, sadness, and disgust. The researchers measured a variety of physiological reactions that accompanied the physical communication of these emotions and found that facial gestures and physiological changes mirrored those of American volunteers. Facial expressions of fear or anger, for example, cause the heart to immediately accelerate for peoples of both cultures.

Movement as Expression

The entire human form, though not as intense an expression of our inner being as the face, can alternately reflect or mask how we really think and feel. "All movements of the human body are expressive, although they may differ in origin and motivation. They may, on the one hand, arise as a direct reflection of mood and inner attitude, as in drumming impatiently with the fingers or leaning forward in eager anticipation; on the other, they may occur in order to fulfill a utilitarian purpose such as moving a chair or digging a garden."*

Movement is consciously used to convey specific themes in endeavors such as dancing, miming and acting. Movement is also expressive, though unconsciously so, when serving more practical ends. Personality is revealed

---

* from *Concepts in Modern Educational Dance* by Betty Redfern, London: Dance Books, 1982.

every time we perform an everyday task or chore. We easily recognize the characteristic poses and mannerisms of friends and loved ones as they walk, sit, and rise. The ways in which people move and carry themselves all spring from a special combination of attributes that make each individual unique.

It is a curious fact that expressive movements bear a close resemblance to motions used in everyday working situations. For example, tapping the fingers to indicate impatience or anxiety is fundamentally the same kind of motion as tapping the keyboard of a computer. Pressing forward in eager anticipation is essentially the same as pushing against a heavy object. In both cases, an action that arises as a result of a particular mood is basically the same as an action employed for a utilitarian purpose.

Laban Notation – Descriptive Variables for Expression

Rudolf Laban identified four basic expressive elements (i.e., space, weight, time and flow) which movement shares with physical reality or nature itself. Using these four elements as descriptors, one can note qualities and patterns in an action sequence and study the motion systematically. Laban Movement Analysis was created so that movements could be documented and saved in the same way that notation can preserve a musical piece. If a dance can be transcribed in this shorthand, then we have a chance of duplicating its magic in later years. Out of this history, Laban Analysis has also come to be used as a language for exchanging information about the ways we move and express ourselves.

Space (in Laban notation) refers to how we move through the medium of space, the patterns that are created, and the relationships to other objects. A movement can be described as direct or indirect in space. *Weight* is the amount of force that is brought to a movement. An action can tend towards being lighter or stronger in terms of its weight. (A variation on weight is that an action can also be on a light/heavy continuum.) *Time* is the quality that notes the rate of change of the action. Rather than fast versus slow, Laban thinks of motion as either staccato or sustained in time. *Flow* refers to the amount of tension retained in the body. Flow describes what is holding you back, and how much. The flow of a movement can tend towards being either more bound or more free.

Laban invokes several rules to make his expressive elements more useful as descriptors. First, all movements fall somewhere in continuums of 'time', 'space', 'weight', and/or 'flow'. For instance, movements that are completely light and entirely lacking in strength are rare. It is much more likely that a movement can be described somewhere between the two poles of light versus strong. Second, these qualities can describe actions that do not have to involve the whole body. An arm movement can be staccato, for instance, while the torso expresses a more sustained quality of motion. Third, the four expressive elements plus effort (described below) can describe complex chains of motion. Fourth, not all of the elements apply to every action. A flick of the wrist, for example, can be light, direct, and staccato, but nondescriptive in terms of flow.

According to Laban, the way these elements are combined in our movement reveals much about our personality. He claims that the mental effort which we exert to make even the slightest movement becomes externalized in physical action. His term, *effort*, denotes the inner source of movement. Fluctuations, combinations, and transitions between qualities of time, space, weight, flow, and effort can describe any individual's movement behavior.

Just as movement can arise as an expression of an inner state, the reverse is also true. Performing certain utilitarian acts can produce corresponding shifts in moods and feelings. **Movement involves change not only of a physical nature but mental and emotional change as well.** It is conceivable that you could become so attuned to the interrelationship between your actions and feelings that motions could be consciously selected to satisfy emotional needs. For example, if you know that typing increases your anxiety level, you can try to avoid that task on days when you are particularly prone to nervousness.

Expressive Therapy

Verbal expression (writing down thoughts and feelings, or sharing them with loved ones or a trusted therapist) clearly demonstrates how communication can help people who dare to express pain that they feel. In grief work, the process of sharing experiences has been hailed as one of the best ways to come to grips with the loss of a loved one. Talking to someone about the loss, writing it down in a journal, or letting the feelings out in some other creative way can help release and relieve the pain of bereavement. Both the suffering and the good times need to be remembered. Sometimes recollections are best expressed in poetry; at other times memories are best left to conversation and/or prose. Expressive therapy can occur through a variety of mediums including art, poetry, dance, drama, or storytelling. With art therapy, clients draw how they feel about a certain situation. Psychodrama involves acting out situations where you want to improve your coping mechanisms. In dance therapy, the task is to find a gesture, pose, or action to express the way the event makes you feel.

Not everything that you express feels good. The childish saying, "Sticks and stones may break my bones, but words will never hurt me," may not be so true in all cases – especially for the person who wields words to express internal rage. Ask yourself how you feel inside when you yell or curse at another person or when you call them names. On the other hand, saying words like 'love', 'peace', 'truth', or 'beauty' out loud often has an uplifting effect. Try a quick experiment and speak these words aloud, and look for any effects they might have on you.

Movement Therapy

Have you ever noticed how infants cry with their whole bodies? They stretch their legs, then suddenly pull back as they circle their arms. For adults too, some emotional conflicts and anxieties can only be kinesthetically expressed . . . they cannot be released any other way. Movement affords an opportunity to acknowledge and let go of these sorts of tensions in a socially acceptable forum. Physical enacting is a powerful way to bring memories and emotions into view. It offers a way to relate to another human being for people who are unable to meaningfully communicate through speech, words, sounds, or pictures.

Skilled physical activity is also a way of asserting self-esteem; an accomplished act says, "I am worthy." When a child succeeds in throwing a ball or riding a bicycle, (s)he gleefully repeats the act again and again. Elizabeth Kübler-Ross tells the story of a child dying from leukemia who requested that he be allowed to stop radiation treatments and go home to ride his bike around the block. Kubler-Ross came home with the boy and made sure the boy's mother let him complete the task all on his own. Although extremely tired, the boy's face radiated with accomplishment as he completed his ride. He died peacefully soon after the event and willed the bike to a brother with the provision that "he never use damn training wheels like I did."

Rituals – Formalized Expression

Humans have developed formalized rituals to express certain aspects of their most personal and meaningful inner reality. These rituals are usually associated with special times in one's life journey such as coming of age, getting married, giving birth or dying, or they help commemorate past events that have symbolism and meaning for the larger culture like Thanksgiving, Christmas, Ramadan, or Passover.

Personal Gestures

Personal gestures help us to express real emotions about something that is personally meaningful. When we plant a tree or visit a memorable place in honor of someone or something, it helps us remember and celebrate the importance of that person or event. Gestures help us sustain a connection between that which is celebrated and us. It is indeed unfortunate when we miss or forget what community rituals stand for. Have you ever attended a funeral when the guests were more interested in gossiping than honoring the dearly departed? Have you partaken of a Thanksgiving meal where no one bothered to offer a prayer of thanks or stopped to consider all the blessings that they were truly grateful for?

Prayerful Movement – Liturgical Dance

Liturgical Dance involves the use of movement in worship, both privately and communally. Those who wished to use their voices in worship have always had a legitimate place in the church through singing and prayer. There is a role for those who play musical instruments in the church. Creative writing talents can be used to forge sermons that inspire parishioners from week to week. There is even a place for those with artistic leanings. They can put together arrangements of flowers on the altar or create other ornamentation for the church. But for the most part, dance is not an accepted part of the weekly service to God. In the recent past, very few if any of the Judeo-Christian sects have integrated movement as a regular part of their religious ceremony. Liturgical dance is still almost unheard of in this day and age.

Yet prayerful movement can be incorporated into almost any part of a traditional worship service: in the processional, along with hymns, even as part of the sermon. In the processional, arm gestures can convey some of the spirit of the day – joyful on a bar mitzvah or Christmas, solemn to pay homage at a funeral or on Palm Sunday. Dance can express more clearly the lyrics of old beloved religious tunes. Gesture and signings can accentuate important parts of the sermon. Mime can illustrate a scripture reading or bible story. Movement can even stand on its own as a special kind of silent holy meditation and prayer.

There are basically only two rules in the performance of liturgical dance. One is not to use dry, meaningless symbolic gestures prescribed by others, but instead to find actions that express your own spirituality. Rule two is to fit the liturgical dance to the congregation. Unlike movement that is only used to express a personal relationship with God, liturgical dance is designed to help a community share in the spirit. So, if you were worshiping with a congregation that tends to shun anything new, you would not begin by performing a free flow interpretation of the scriptures. A gentler way of introducing movement into the ceremony might be to incorporate simple participatory arm and hand movements as an accompaniment to one of the day's hymns.

Gurdjieff 'Movements' are designed to spark an awareness of something higher and to evoke an emotional response to complex motor demands. These movements are precisely defined positions of the hands, arms, feet, legs, and head, sometimes with voice participation. They are performed in changing formations to specially composed melodies, which further enhance the emotional and spiritual response felt by the dancers. Often, the maneuvers are so complex that one cannot perform them without giving up worrying about what (s)he is doing. Practitioners bring an inordinate amount of attention to the task of remembering and executing the difficult routines. Even with such concentration and effort, the difficulty of the movements is such that they could not be executed without relying on 'something higher'. When Gurdjieff movements are performed with attention on this elevated spirit they take on an almost holy quality.

Body Work

1. *Body Mapping characteristic feelings, thoughts and moods.* This exercise can take a great deal of time and attention, or you can spend as little time on it as you want. The rewards of Body Mapping are cumulative. The idea is to create a road map of your unique personal body signals. Whenever you catch yourself expressing a habitual emotion or attitude such as, "People with money can't be trusted," notice the shape of your body and any physical sensations . . . is your jaw clenched or do you feel hungry? A careful survey of this kind can help you to recognize body signals that have special significance for you, such as "My stomach always bothers me when I'm angry." By comparing notes with friends, you may discover characteristics which tend to be shared and other traits which are distinctly 'you'.

2. *Brightening habitual modes of expression.* Sanaya Roman suggests that you can cancel negative impressions received from others with more

affirmative images of your own. To do so, you must first listen to your conversations as if you were an eavesdropper. Do your friends habitually use words that uplift you, or do they speak in terms that strike a disagreeable or uneasy chord? If you would like to brighten the energy of a conversation, interject thoughts silently or aloud that are high and loving and watch for a change. For example, if you hear something like "The world is a frightening place," and you do not want to take part in this image, say to yourself, "The world is a joyful place."

3. *Increasing joy through verbal expression.* As an extension of the last exercise, try this easy variation. For each letter of the alphabet, think of the most uplifting word you can. Speak each word out loud. Notice how you feel after speaking each of these positive words. You can also play this game in the car, by looking at license plates and creating words out of the letters you see.

4. *Increasing joy through movement.* Take the list of terms that you discovered in playing the previous exercise and create a different movement to symbolize each word. Your motions should express moods, feelings and thoughts that the word evokes in you. Move your body in different ways to show: joy, peace, love, truth, and any other concept that you care to kinesthetically explore.

5. *Increasing awareness of the expressive qualities of movement – Laban Movement Analysis.* Choose two activities that you are likely to engage in this week (e.g., washing dishes, talking on the phone, writing letters). Categorize each activity using Laban elements of time, weight, space and flow. Are your movements quick or sustained, light or strong, indirect or direct, bound or free? For instance, if I select 'talking on the phone', I might note that it is a 'sustained' and 'bound' action. (Notice that not all elements are applicable to every action.) Does this kind of assessment tell you anything new about the way you perform these commonplace behaviors? Does it help you see why you do or do not like your chosen activities?

6. *Creating your own rituals.* Celebrate a special day by creating a new ritual, a formal recognition of an event. Your celebration should honor something meaningful in your life that, heretofore, has not been formally

recognized. You could commemorate, for instance, the day you learned to ride a bike. Your gesture could be biking five miles on a lovely trail with a good friend to share the pleasure of the day. See how creatively you can express the meaningfulness of this special event.

* * * * *

Play is one of the most natural ways of acting out and expressing all of the conflicting feelings and thoughts that haunt our souls. It is one avenue we have for 'letting it all hang out'. Play is doing *what you want to do* rather than doing *what you are supposed to do*. Doing what you really want helps you to discover what you are all about, what makes you unique, what makes you, 'you'. Play and movement have a synergistic relationship; becoming more fluent in one can help you to better understand the other. You can explore the intriguing relationship for yourself in the next chapter on **play**.

Chapter 9

PLAY

*Life must be lived as play, playing certain games,
making sacrifices, singing and dancing, and then a
man will be able to propitiate the gods.*
– Plato

It's all right to have a good time.
*– Thaddeus Golas, in The Lazy Man's Guide to
Enlightenment*

One of the most wonderful features of humanity is our propensity for play. Children and a few lighthearted adults seem to know that it is truly all right to have a good time.

Grown-Ups Dismiss Play as Unproductive

As men and women enter what is commonly known as the 'productive' years (usually around the ages of 21 to 55), they tend to lose sight of play as a worthwhile pursuit. It is my observation that adults in general do not play as long or as well as children do. Perhaps it is because we get so caught up in duties and obligations that we forget the inherent value in play. Perhaps without practice we simply forget how to have fun. Regardless of the reason, what I see is that grown-ups (I wonder, does the name imply that 'grown-ups' have no more growing to do?) convert action into effort and try too hard to accomplish arbitrary feats. As adults, we are so busy struggling for perfection that we leave precious little time or energy for play. When we realize that we aren't doing anything that we enjoy, we work too hard at trying to have fun. As an example of this phenomenon, I point to the ubiquitous jogger with a grim and determined look on the face as (s)he grinds out a daily run in sizzling hot, sub-zero cold, or monsoon wet weather. Or what about the aerobics fanatic who isn't happy unless (s)he is injured from overexertion and 'going for the burn'. These over-avid sports enthusiasts show us how, if you go out and work at playing really, really hard, you can spoil any amount of fun and screw yourself up in the bargain. Another obstacle that hampers our natural playfulness is the fear of looking foolish. Adolescents and young adults, in particular, are especially susceptible to sacrificing happiness for self-image. They are constantly critiquing and criticizing their performances. Unfortunately for them, the strategy of avoiding anything that might make one look foolish is not sound. If you are unwilling to make mistakes, if you must master a technique on the first try, how can you possibly learn anything new?

Letting Go

Happily, it appears that most people regain a capacity for play as they grow past the ages of 20, 30, 40 and into wisdom. A key ingredient of play is letting go. Older men and women tend to remember what the important aspects of life are, and are willing to let go of those that aren't so important.

Barriers – Social Restrictions

Movement is an invaluable aid in helping acquire the skill and artistry of letting go. But just knowing that movement is a tool is not enough. We need to allow ourselves the freedom to indulge in motion. Ask yourself, how often do you allow your body to let go? How often are you free to move any way that you want? How often do you feel the freedom to indulge your body in its kinesthetic whims? When your neck feels tight while you wait in the supermarket checkout line, will you give yourself permission to stretch out the tightness with a couple of neck rolls or shoulder shrugs? Or do you suffer in silence? If you are in an incredibly boring meeting chaired by your boss, do you stifle your yawns and the urge to squirm? Due to social restrictions, most likely you will limit your movements to those that seem appropriate to the situation.

Barriers – Habits

Social restrictions on movement are magnified by habitual restrictions that we place on ourselves. Since we are not used to stretching without our customary stretching gear, we won't indulge without wearing a leotard and sweats. Letting go of the largely internal rules and regulations that we place upon ourselves carries us a long way towards freedom. We become freer to do the things that make us unique and special. We become freer to do what we really want. After all, it is quite doubtful that at the end of a lifetime you will be concerned about the report that didn't get done, or the house that wasn't cleaned as well as you would have liked.

Instead of always turning playtime into work, perhaps it would be well to see if we could turn our workaday time into play. This does not mean we should address responsibilities as frivolous and unimportant. It simply means that it might be helpful to bring the energy and joy that we find in play to all of our activities. But first we must rediscover how we play.

In this regard, once again movement can be an excellent teacher. Moving the body just to see what happens is play. Maneuvering the body to see what feels good is enjoyable. Shifting the body in certain ways just to see if you can do it is fun. Movement captures the essence of play. Doing something for the sheer joy of it, because you like to do it, because you enjoy it – that is play. You do not need a special reason to justify moving and you do not need a special reason to justify play. Enjoyment is a valid enough reason in itself.

Humor

Almost unconsciously, we use humor to ease ourselves in times of depression, anxiety and stress. Norman Cousins used humor in a more dramatic way and found that, for him, ten minutes of laughter translated into two hours of painless sleep. He used laughing to combat the usually fatal disease of ankylosing spondylitis (disintegration of spinal connective tissue).

Recreation

Sometimes we call our playtime "recreation." **Recreation** is just what it sounds like . . . to create all over again. By concentrating on having fun, in a way we are creating ourselves and our world anew. We become ourselves, but new. After spending time in recreational activities, we find ourselves fresh and better able to deal with the challenges of everyday life. Good recreation always leaves us feeling that we can take on the world.

Part and parcel of the natural propensity towards play and recreation is the natural propensity to create. Just as we all have the ability to play, all of us are naturally creative. But many times we do not give ourselves credit for our creative acts. When you figure out how to fix an old piece of furniture, you are being creative. When you think up a game to amuse a child, you are making something totally original and new. When you see images and shapes in the form of a cloud, in a sense, you are creating them. There are countless more examples of creativity in everyone's daily life.

One of the benefits of being creative and recognizing the quality of creativity in yourself is that it makes you feel good. Creativity improves mental health and self-image. It can also make problems easier to solve, relationships more rewarding, and days packed with fun. When you encourage innovation, you become more and more of the kind of person you like to know and be.

Creativity can be enhanced in anyone. Many of us fail to realize that creativity and play are skills that can be practiced and improved. They are not inner talents that a person either does or does not possess. It is not the case that you cannot play because you do not have the talent. Like any skill, practice can improve your capacity for having fun. Without practice, your creative and playful aspects wither and die.

Researchers have identified four components of creativity that can be enhanced with practice. These are fluency, flexibility, elaboration, and originality.

Fluency is the ability to come up with many different solutions to a problem. Brainstorming is one way to develop fluency. The idea is to take a problem and come up with as many solutions as you can. Brainstorming is often practiced in a group situation. The only caution is not to choose or criticize any of the answers until you have finished generating them. Don't worry about whether the solutions are practical or even possible – the goal is to free up the mind so that inspiration will flow.

Flexibility is the capacity to look at situations from a different point of view. (See Chapter 4 for more information and exercises to develop **flexibility**.)

Elaboration is adding on to an already existing solution. When we embellish or refine a theory, we are elaborating.

Many people think of *originality* as being a synonym for creativity. It certainly is an integral component. Originality is the ability to come up with a completely new, never-before-tried idea. Inventors do this when they create innovative products. Some famous inventions that demonstrate originality are packaged seeds, hula-hoops, electric light bulbs, and the slinky.

Letting the body play can enhance all of these features: originality, elaborating, flexibility, and fluency. You can entertain yourself and others for hours by making a game out of, "What does my body like to do?" How many original ways can you find to move across a room, for instance? Attempting to experientially answer this question will build both originality and fluency skills. To strengthen elaborative skills, pose a testable kinesthetic challenge. For instance, how could you elaborate on the act of twirling your partner?

Playacting and Imagination

Think back to the games you loved to play when you were a child. I suspect that the vast majority of your playtime was spent in fantasy. Children play and learn by imagining themselves in a multitude of situations . . . everything from pretending to be a mommy or a daddy, to cowboys and Indians, to space pilots and astronauts, to playing doctor. As adults, we do not ordinarily allow ourselves to indulge in such childish imaginings. However, we still love to be entertained with the fantasy world enacted by professional entertainers. We will pay substantial sums of money to attend the theater to see a 'play'. Modern day heroes tend to be actors, singers, sports stars, or other entertainment figures – people we designate to do the playing for the rest of us. No doubt, we receive a benefit from the vicarious pleasure of watching actors play or pretend. But think how much greater the reward would be if we would begin to pretend again for ourselves.

Imagining as Therapy

Imagery has been used to alter destructive attitudes, behaviors and even diseases like cancer. Visualization was first used as a tool for dealing with problems of the psyche (e.g., phobias, neuroses, and anxiety). More recently, imagery has been incorporated into therapies designed to restore, protect, and enhance physical health (e.g., pain and nausea reduction treatments for cancer).

Hypnosis

One of the first clinical uses for imagery was Mesmer's discovery of hypnosis (also called mesmerism), an artificially-induced sleeplike state in which the subject is highly susceptible to suggestion. Hypnosis has been successfully used to diminish such things as smoking, the pain and nausea associated with cancer, and bedwetting.

Systematic Desensitization

Also known as *reciprocal inhibition*, systematic desensitization helps people overcome anxieties and phobias step-by-step. Patients remain in a relaxed state (induced by Progressive Muscular Relaxation) while they are cued to imagine a series of increasingly anxiety-provoking situations (i.e., a hierarchy of fears that the client has developed). By the end of a desensitization, patients are able to stay relaxed while imagining even the stimulus that they are most afraid of. Emotive imagery is a variation on desensitization that is especially helpful with children. Children imagine a story into which the therapist introduces feared objects.

Forward Time Projection (FTP)

FTP helps put anxiety in perspective and relieves tension over impending events. The technique involves imagining a situation that is bothering you now and trying to envision the situation as it will be in the future. For example, if I were anxious about upcoming surgery, I would first visualize myself getting prepared for the operation, then feeling relieved immediately after the surgery, and finally feeling well and happy six months later.

Psychodrama

This form of therapy involves acting out personal problems in a group setting. Role-playing can serve as practice for upcoming events or as a tool for understanding past problems.

Placebos

Health practitioners recognize the efficacy of substances with no known pharmacological action in combating ulcers, warts, vomiting, and nausea and also in the alleviation of post-operative pain, seasickness, headaches, coughs, and anxiety. It is believed that these placebos work by triggering healing visualizations. When a patient believes a 'drug' will heal, it does.

Visualization

The Simontons used visualization to treat some cancers. Patients relax and imagine a peaceful scene, then 'see' the cancer being broken up or 'eaten' by their immune system – sometimes in the form of little 'pac men' – and flushed away.

Bates developed a number of visualization exercises for improving vision. He based his work on the observation that sight involves both a sense impression from the eye and an interpretation of the impression by the brain. Bates encouraged patients to conjure up images they enjoyed, like peaceful scenes from nature, in order to relax their eyes. In another exercise, subjects visualize total blackness to soothe the eyes and mind.

Auto-suggestion and Autogenic training

Sub-verbal suggestion and body-oriented visualizations are used to induce relaxation and as an adjunctive therapy for ulcers, gall bladder attacks, hypertension, headaches, asthma, diabetes, arthritis, and low back pain.

Imagery and Movement

Mental Practice is the mental rehearsal of a physical activity without an accompanying gross motor response. Richardson's classic experiment studied the effects of imagery in shooting free throws. One group of students physically practiced free throws faithfully every day for twenty consecutive days. The second group had no practice. The last group also had no intervening practice, but spent twenty minutes a day visualizing themselves sinking free throws. The practicing and visualizing groups both showed an improvement of 23% after twenty days while the non-practicing, non-visualizing group stayed the same.

Trager Psychophysical Integration

Milton Trager developed a bodywork system based on the notion that pleasurable movement is the most effective teacher.

Trager movements, called Mentastics, exemplify the quality of playfulness. The name, Mentastics, intentionally blends the word 'mental' with 'gymnastics'. Mentastics are light, simple ways of moving that create awareness, improve function, and recall a feeling of lightness and freedom. The actions remind me of a constantly fluttering wave motion. This motion gives information about the body to the 'functional mind', which uses the data to relieve unnecessary tensions and pain. The 'functional mind' is that part of your mind that takes over the function of complex motor tasks after they have been learned. Driving, swimming, and riding a bike are all handled by the functional mind. Everyday motor tasks such as these would be excruciating if we had to consciously review each step as it was completed.

Trager table work consists of gentle stretching, rhythmic rocking, and shaking motions. The client's responses guide the bodyworker, who is trained to be more concerned with creating a pleasant sensation of lightness and flexibility than with kneading out tension. The therapist concentrates on just how light and free the body can feel and his/her hands transmit that sensation to the patient. Experiencing the lightness is known as 'hook up'. 'Hook up' is a sensation of being in the now, experiencing, listening and feeling.

For both Mentastics and the table work, light easy movements generate pleasurable sensory signals, which, in turn, release tensions brought on by trauma, illness, or emotional wounds. Increased sensory awareness is said to increase an awareness of the relationship between body and mind, too. Consider the images of a baseball bat, a feather, and a fly. Imagine that in one hand you hold the bat and in the other you hold the feather. Let's say a fly comes into the room and is about to land on one of the objects. Are you better able to distinguish the difference in weight if the fly rests on the bat or on the feather? I would hazard a guess that the change would be easier to perceive if the fly were to land on the feather. Just so, when your body feels as light as a feather, you become more aware of physical stimuli acting upon you.

Body Work

1. *Pretend play.* Pretending to be an animal. There are several variations on this group exercise.

    a) In the first variation, the leader names an animal from a list and all participants act as if they were that animal. How would you move if you were a cat, dog, lion, chicken, beetle, bee, deer, snake, snail, monkey, squirrel, horse, jaguar, owl, or butterfly?

    b) Choose the animal that moves its body most similarly to the way you move. Write the name down on a slip of paper. If you are going to do part (c), put the paper aside for now. If not, go on and move as if you had become your chosen animal. Do the movements fit? Why did you choose this particular animal?

    c) This variation requires a group of people who are familiar with each other, and who have seen each other do physical work. Each participant receives as many slips of paper as there are remaining people in the group. On each slip of paper, write the name of one of your comrades and the animal that (s)he most reminds you of. When you are finished, distribute the papers to the appropriate comrades and leave them lying face down. Everyone should end up with one less slip than there are people in the group. Now comes the fun part. Read the animals that others have chosen to represent you and take turns acting out the parts. Everyone else tries to guess what animals are being portrayed. As each person finishes his animal repertoire, the others can tell why they selected the animals that they did.

2. *Mentastics.* Trager movements embody the essence of easy play. Here are a few sample movements to intensify the feelings of lightness, ease, and being in the now. As you try each motion, remind yourself in a gentle

way to ask "What could be lighter?" "What could be easier?" and "How can I move in a gentler way?"

a) Begin by simply picking up the right hand and letting it fall like a feather. Can it fall more lightly or gently? Add a little butterfly flutter to your motion. Can you sense a tingling in your arm as nerve connections to the brain are activated?

b) Now shake both hands lightly in front of your face, overhead, then down at your sides. Trager disciples lovingly call this movement Trager applause.

c) Now let your whole body move around any way that it wants to. Give attention to the lightness and ease with which you move. Continue in this 'cosmic dance' for a few minutes or so. Does your body feel more playful and alive? Can you sense the blood flow in your arms and legs? And most importantly, were you having fun?

3. *Creativity*. One way to enhance creativity and to have some fun doing it, is to play the dictionary game. To start the game, one person finds a word in the dictionary that no one else knows. The rest make up definitions for the word that sound as if they could be real. They write these fake definitions down and hand them over to the person who chose the word, while the chooser writes down the real definition. The person with the dictionary reads all of the definitions including the real one, and the rest of the group votes for the most likely definition. You get a point if anyone votes for your made up definition or if you pick the correct one. The winner is the one with the most points when the game is called. It may be surprising to see how closely some of your definitions match each other and/or the real definition of the word. If you wish to play this game with pre-made slips of paper and preselected words, you can purchase it under the trade name *Balderdash*.

4. *Synthesis*. Putting two parts together and creating something new – two parts of a dance. For this experience, pair up with a partner. Each will work separately, then together. First, everyone creates a four-count combination of movements. One partner devises upper body and arm movements while the other creates lower body and leg positions. Combinations can be as simple as one pose held for four counts, or they can

be as complex as four (or more, so long as the motions follow a regular beat) different movements. Demonstrate and teach your combination to your partner. Allow your partner to do the same for you. Finally, combine the two combinations into a four-count whole body combination that uses both arms and legs. Demonstrate the new synthesized work for the rest of the group. How is it received?

5. *Imaginings.* Imagine yourself with everything that you could possibly want: your perfect job, relationship, house and your perfect you. Remember to make these images of things that you really want (e.g., usually you want money to fulfill some other wish, like freedom from work, security, or travel). What would a typical day be like if you had everything that you wanted? What would you need to do to get these imaginings for real? Are you willing to pay the price? If not, you may want to revise the images you are hoping for.

*   *   *   *   *

When we learn to free ourselves up enough to play, it is not long before we yearn for someone to play with us. We seek the company of other human beings to share our joys and our sorrows, our laughter and our pain. We reach out to other physical entities and form relationships. Emotional and intellectual bonds have a real counterpart on the physical level. The ramifications of these kinesthetic 'connections' are explored in the next chapter on **relationships**.

Chapter 10

RELATIONSHIPS

No man is an island entire of itself; every man is a
piece of the continent, a part of the main . . .
– John Donne

Everyone and everything is interconnected and
interrelated.
– Joseph DiRende, in Harmonious Living

All of human life is connected. Humans have relationships to everyone
and everything. We have a special bond with the parents who gave us
life and nurtured our growth. We have developed associations with each
of our teachers. We have created intimate relationships with friends and
lovers. We even have an association of sorts with many people we do
not choose to spend time with. Strangers who happen to meet our eye
while passing in the street are in some kind of relationship to us. We also
have links to objects such as food, alcoholic beverages, and our jobs.

Primary Relationship is with Ourselves

Of all the connections we forge in our lives, by far the most important
is the relationship we have with ourselves. Associations that you have
made with food and objects and other people all reflect the relationship
you have developed with yourself. Krishnamurti, a 20th century spiritual
teacher, said, "Relationship is surely the mirror in which you discover
yourself." For myself, I have indeed found that my relationships with
others mirror different facets of my personality. These parts of myself

I might never have seen if it weren't for my interactions with others. The people I invite into my life reflect parts of me so that I can see myself in a new way. In one friend, who is a university professor, I see the teacher in me. By observing her situation, I can see some of the same difficulties that I have experienced in the role of teacher, but in a more objective, and less emotional way. Another friend is always gruff and hard on himself. It is much easier for me to accept the gruff and harder side of myself when I see it reflected in my friend.

Sometimes the love and respect we wish we were getting from the outside world is the love and respect we need to learn to give ourselves. Sometimes the fear of being abandoned is because we abandon ourselves. Our connection to ourselves is truly the key to our connections with the outside world. So each of us must ask ourselves, "What kind of relationship have I created with myself?" Do you enjoy the time you spend in your own company, or do you feel edgy when forced to be alone?

How Relationships are Formed – Organization and Coordination

When we examine a functioning system, we observe elements joined in such a way that everything works together more or less smoothly. When parts are united in this way, we say the whole is coordinated and organized. The body is an excellent example. A functioning whole human being is made up of organ systems (e.g., digestive, respiratory, muscular, skeletal). Each organ system has a purpose and contributes to the well-being of the whole. For example, the skeletal system acts as a support for the entire body. Coordination and organization in the body also exist below the level of human individual as functioning system. Just as each individual body is served by organ systems, each organ system is comprised of individual organs, all performing important and specialized functions. The digestive system, for example, is served by the mouth, esophagus, stomach, small and large intestines. Each organ has a vital role in sustaining the digestive system. The mouth chews the food and a ptyalin enzyme in the mouth helps break down carbohydrates. The stomach acts as an acid bath to help digest proteins and other molecules that have gotten that far in the digestive system without breaking down. The small intestine is the main vehicle for absorbing and distributing nutrients. The large intestine absorbs water and concentrates waste matter to be excreted.

Focusing on still smaller systems, we note that each organ is integrated into a unit from cells. Every cell is a unit with vital coordinated parts. Cellular components are molecules and molecules are formed from atoms. Modern science has even confirmed the existence of subatomic particles. At this juncture, scientists do not even know how infinitesimally small an organized human system could be.

Synthesis

In the examples above, we explored units that were coordinated into functioning wholes by synthesis. The Greek prefix 'syn' means 'together with'. Synthesis means creating something by combining together with others that are not the same as us. Cooperation, integration, and creativity all result from such a process. Examine the kinds of words that result from using the prefix, 'syn-': 'synthesis' means 'putting together'; 'synergy' means 'working together'; 'syntropy' means 'being together'.

Synthesis is the putting together of unlike individual units. When you combine two different foods, for example, you come up with a dish that is unique. When things and people come together something new and wonderful happens. In relationship there is creativity, complexity, richness, and a spark of something new. Whether we are talking about recipes or sports teams, an organized whole is more than the parts that make it up. In other words, to modify a proposition from applied mathematics, a synthesized whole is greater than the sum of its parts.

Unison

A whole can also be organized from parts that all adopt the same function. In this case, members work together in unison. True unity seems to engender a feeling of agreement and support. There is a special pleasure that we derive from working in unison. In this simplest case of organization, every part of the group is working in tandem with all the other members. In a certain way we become the same as our fellows.

Moving or singing or doing anything in unison involves a willingness to adapt one's activities and behaviors in order to fit in with a grander design. "United we stand and divided we fall" becomes a motto for a unison group project. There is a sense that a greater purpose may be accomplished with unity than can be achieved with a focus on individualism and disharmony. Unison creates a feeling of expansion and openness. It allows the focus to be addressed outward.

Working together as one utilizes imitation. The simplicity of having every person repeat the same phrase allows everyone to concentrate on similarities rather than differences. Each participant can focus on and direct attention to making their own movements, songs, or chants more like the parts played by comrades. In essence, a group focus requires each member to deaccentuate and deemphasize their individual characters. Unison group movement requires members to see how their motions are different and to modify those differences for the sake of the whole.

Support

Support from others fosters a sense of belonging, of being needed, and of being loved. Having people you feel close with and whom you can really talk to is a most satisfying human phenomenon. Research has shown that people who can talk to family or friends about their problems are more emotionally and physiologically healthy. People who support you want to share your joys, problems, hopes and fears. Family, friends, lovers, counselors, or anyone who accepts you for who you are can provide social support. Social support is being accepted "for oneself and not for what one can do."

One of the keys to developing a wider support system is being open and caring with others. It is often easier and less threatening to stay aloof and detached. Fear prevents us from getting close. We fear that we may be rejected, embarrassed or ridiculed, if we show our love. We may even fear that we are not able to love another person. To develop social support, one must be willing to give as well as receive.

Intimate Relationships

Some people believe that sexual bonding is the same as intimacy. While expressing sexuality with another human being can be an intimate experience, sometimes (as much as we would like it to be), it isn't. Intimacy more properly describes a bond that is very strong and lasting. That kind of deep connection may or may not occur in tandem with physical expression. At any rate, it is not sexual intimacy alone that creates true intimacy. I believe that intimate relationships are built up from shared experiences. Shared activities can be physical (having sex, swimming, or taking a walk with a friend) or they can focus on more emotional (sharing secrets), intellectual (taking the same class), or spiritual (sharing a belief in a higher power, attending the same church) experiences. When connections run very deep and ties have been established on many levels, we say that a relationship is intimate.

Relating to the Body

Although we do not relate to others wholly on a corporeal level, the way we feel about our own bodies greatly influences the way we think about ourselves in relationship to other people. For many of us, the relationship with our own body is not a good one. In a recent anecdotal study of female college students, I found not one single student who could identify a body part that she admired (or would admit to admiring). Yet there were plenty of body parts that were disliked. Hips were high on the list of out-of-favor zones, along with stomachs and thighs. It is difficult to understand what would make these young women in the prime of vitality ashamed of their beautiful, strong, healthy bodies. The primary strategy they devised for dealing with problem areas was to get rid of the excess . . .

to diet it off. These college coeds seemed to genuinely hate their bodies. They just wanted their 'bad' parts to go away. After hearing so many negative attitudes about body image, I wondered how these young women could ever learn to create a better relationship with their bodily selves.

Listening to Corporeal Cues

As is true in any relationship, communication is the most useful skill for improving our relationship to our bodies. Can we hear what our body is saying? Do we listen to what it likes and dislikes? Do we respect those choices? If the answer to any of these queries is 'no', then we will need to boost our listening skills and/or learn to respect the body more.

In our society, it is commonplace to ignore the body and think that its needs are unimportant. When the mind says, "I must" meet this job deadline and the body says, "I'm tired" or "I'm hungry", invariably it is the body that is shortchanged. Or when the stomach cries, "I'm full" at Thanksgiving but the eyes crave a little more turkey, dressing and pie, it is usually the stomach that has to find a way of dealing with excess food. With desk jobs, long car commutes, and watching television as our major leisure pastimes, we rarely exercise or even stretch when the body feels cramped. Planning our lives by a strict schedule dictated by appointments and meetings, we rarely stop to rest when we feel physically fatigued. Still our bodies continue to perform, doing all that is necessary to keep us functional and alive. The body will carry on as a faithful servant, even after we ignore its pleas, desires, and needs, until it becomes physically unable to function. The body finally succumbs to the effects of stress and we become ill. Unless we learn to listen to our corporeal messages, this kind of scenario is inevitable.

Since listening to the body is not something we habitually do, we must practice. Working with any of the Body Work exercises in Chapter 1 on **awareness** will help attune these skills. There are two logical approaches to becoming more sensitive to physical needs. One is to deny the body something that you know it wants, but doesn't need, like drinking sodas or coffee. This could also involve forcing the body to do something it doesn't want to do, like keeping both feet on the floor whenever you sit down. Before long, there will be an inner protest and you can clearly hear what the body (and mind) has to say about the matter. When the denial is severe, the inner voice will actually shout its dissent. This is the way of the fakir or the celibate and I do not recommend it as a basis for scientific exploration. There is too much danger that denial will become habitual and physically destructive (e.g., chronic dieting that shifts into life-threatening anorexia nervosa).

The second way of sharpening listening skills is more gentle and the results more subtle. On the down side, it takes more concentration to practice and to notice a change. This approach involves valuing the body enough to pay attention to all of the little aches or rumbles that it makes. This technique would quickly become overwhelming if you tried to focus on the entire body every minute of the day. If we lighten the task, it will make it easier to succeed. So, set aside just five minutes each day to focus on what your body wants to do, and do it! If your body feels like lying down during those five minutes, lie down. If a finger wants to jiggle, let it jiggle. If you want to scowl, if you want to grin, if you want to run, jump, or skip . . . for that interval of time, whatever your body wants, do it. Your physical body will be eternally grateful for the attention and you may learn some very valuable things about what the body needs and wants in the process.

Wholistic Health

Relating to others involves seeing oneself as part of a whole. More and more health care professionals and laypersons alike are realizing that the wholistic perspective is the healthiest one. Consider the words 'hale' and 'healthy'. Both are related to the term, 'whole'. Modern society is beginning to recognize this important connection as evidenced by the proliferation of wholistic health services. Such interventions treat people as whole human beings, not just as symptoms such as sprained ankles or cancerous growths.

Hatha Yoga

Yoga is one of the oldest wholistic health disciplines still practiced today. The word 'yoga' literally means 'to join together' or 'to yoke'. We can think of the joining as union of body and mind, or as union of self with others, or as union of self with something higher, like God or Spirit. Raja yoga, the eight-fold path, includes a ladder of teachings from all paths of yoga. The eight angas (rungs) of the ladder are yamas (restraints), niyamas (observances), asanas (postures), pranayama (control of breath), pratyahara (control of the senses), dharana (concentration), dhyana (meditation) and samadhi (like nirvana, a superconscious state). In Hatha Yoga, the focus is on the union of body and mind. Pranayama is coordinated with asanas. As you breathe in, your body expands and as you breathe out it contracts. Joining the breath with movement is crucial. When breathing works in conjunction with bodily effort, the mind is calmed and physical action is easier and more relaxed.

Body Work

1. *Unison*
   a) The exercise begins with a group of three or more in a cluster, all facing the same direction. The person who seems to be at the head of the group begins to move. The others move in unison with the leader.
   b) As the facing direction of the movement and therefore the group changes, so does the leader. Always the person who cannot see any of the others becomes the leader. As you move in unison with the group, what feelings are engendered in you? Are they feelings of collegiality or compassion? Or are they feelings of competition and judgment of yourself or others? When someone in the group misses a step, how does that make you feel? When you take your turn as the leader, do your feelings change?

2. *Synthesis and Coordination – Making a machine that works*
   a) This is one of those games that counselors like to play in summer

camp. One person (A) begins by moving as if (s)he were a part of a machine. (S)he makes a repeating motion and (optionally) an accompanying repetitive noise. The second person (B) enters and connects up with the first cog. For example, Person B enters and puts a hand on Person A's hip. Person B repeats his/her own signature motion (and sound) over and over again. Person C joins the group in a similar way and the pattern continues until everyone in the group becomes part of the machine. What kind of machine did your group create? What part did you play? What kind of cog did you become?

b) In this variation the machine must be mobile. It must be able to move as a whole at each step of its construction and when it is complete. Each cog still contributes a repeating action (and sound). Does mobility alter the quality of the machine? If so, how is it different from the one that was fixed in place?

3. *Trust exercises*

a) You need a partner for this exercise, preferably someone you do not already know and trust. One person in each twosome closes the eyes or wears a blindfold. The other is responsible for leading the 'blind' partner through space. This should be done slowly at first. When safety allows, the leader can guide the partner into more daring movement, such as running, waltzing, or sitting and rising. After five minutes have elapsed, change roles. How did you feel about this partner? Did you trust him/her? Can you remember if the feeling shifted as the exercise progressed? When you played the role of leader, how did it feel to be responsible for someone else's safety? Can you remember feeling different about your partner at the outset of this activity?

b) This is a variation of exercise (a). You need several twosomes for this version. In this situation, any leader may exchange 'blind' partners with any other leader at any time. Followers keep their eyes closed or wear a blindfold so that they do not know who is leading them. Apply the questions that were posed in part (a) to this experience.

c) One person stands in the middle of a circle with eyes closed. This person's feet are together and arms are crossed over the chest. Other members of the group stand in a circle surrounding the center with shoulders almost touching. Someone begins by gently pushing the individual in the middle in any direction. The middle person's body holds rigid as the feet move in response to each push. Everyone else's job is to push or twist the center person around the circle. Everyone is responsible for not letting this person fall. After about five minutes, someone else assumes the center position. When everyone has taken a turn in the middle, answer the following questions. Did you trust the people who pushed you around the circle? What was it like on the outside of the circle? How did you feel when it looked as if the center person might fall?

4. *Bull's-eye.* On a piece of paper, as big or small as you like, draw a bull's-eye. Draw a center core and concentric rings that radiate out from the center. Label the figure, 'My Relationships'. Starting in the core, write in names that are core relationships. Core relationships are people you can call at 3 a.m., without reservation, who will automatically respond, "Of course, I'll be there in a minute." These kinds of relationships are rare. Sometimes while we are learning how to have core relationships, therapists perform the bull's-eye role. Sometimes a family member or an old boyfriend is our main support. Core relationships tend to be free and easy and not dependent at all. There is no feeling of needing these people. Sometimes in the core is a friend who lives 3,000 miles away whom we never see and always forget to call. We occasionally remember to send a card or email that says, "I love you so much. I'm so sorry I haven't written." Then another ten years go by . . . because there is no need. A loving relationship is forever present and whenever you connect, it ignites.

Outer rings have to do with needs. These circles have more difficulty involved, more work. The ring closest to the core usually has to do with romantic or family connections. We wish these people could be in the core. We're always trying to find some way of putting them there. And we're always getting hung up in some way that keeps them from being in the core.

Casual acquaintances, like the person you play golf with, reside close to the outer-most ring. The outermost ring is for the mailman, checkers at the grocery store, and folks on the street who smile at you when you don't even know their names.

This exercise helps you see where your relationships really are, not how you would like them to be. The bull's-eye helps you sort out the connections you need from those you wish to impose. That kind of clarity can help lighten all relationships.

5. *Support.* Use the cantilever exercise on p.80 (4).

*   *   *   *   *

One of the most rewarding aspects of relationships is the ability to touch others on a deep level. When we touch, we open ourselves to sensing and being sensed. Simultaneously, we allow ourselves to feel a separate entity and allow another human being to contact us physically, emotionally, and spiritually. **Touch** allows us to remember that although we exist as separate beings we are still connected. The next chapter allows us to investigate the connections we forge through this most corporeal of the senses . . . our physical sense of **touch**.

Chapter 11

TOUCH
The Physical Sense

When you come to be sensibly touched, the scales will fall from your eyes; and by the penetrating eyes of love you will discern that which your other eyes will never see.
— Francois Fenelon

Our skin contains receptors for sensing and is linked by sensory nerves to the brain, either directly or through the spinal cord. In certain parts of the body this mechanism is especially refined. The palmar surfaces of the hand, for instance, take in extremely subtle stimuli and transmit enormous amounts of information to the brain. When humans are forced to use touch as their primary knowing mode, they realize just how valuable sensory data can be. A blind person, for example, can read Braille with the fingers or choose a given coin out of a pocket by touch.

Touch as a Way to Gather Information

Touch is the most intimate way that we physically sense and make sense of our world. Handling, fingering, probing, and stroking allow us to scrutinize our world in a particularly human way. Of all the external senses, touch is the first to develop. As babies, it is primarily through tactile experience that we explore and make sense of our environment.

Jacques Lusseyran talks at length about the use of touch as a way to exchange information with the physical world in his book, *And There*

Was Light. Lusseyran went blind at the age of eight and subsequently recovered his sight as an adult, so he knows firsthand about the validity of tactile experience. When reflecting upon his first use of the hands as a primary vehicle for observation, he describes the experience in the following way, "At first my hands refused to obey. When they looked for a glass on the table, they missed it. They fumbled around the door knobs, mixed up black and white keys at the piano, fluttered in the air as they came near things . . . Fortunately, before long I realized that instead of becoming useless they were learning to be wise . . . I had thought they (my hands) were refusing to obey, but it was all because they were not getting orders when the eyes were no longer there to command them. But more than that it was a question of rhythm. Our eyes run over the surfaces of things. All they require is a few scattered points, since they can bridge the gap in a flash. They 'half see' much more than they see, and they never weigh. They are satisfied with appearances, and for them the world glows and slides by, but lacks substance. Movement of the fingers was terribly important . . . My fingers felt the pulsation (of objects) distinctly, and if they failed to answer with a pulsation of their own, the fingers immediately became helpless and lost their sense of touch. But when they went toward things, in sympathetic vibration with them, they recognized them right away. Yet there was something still more important than movement, and that was pressure. If I put my hand on the table without pressing it, I knew the table was there, but knew nothing about it. To find out, my fingers had to bear down, and the amazing thing is that the pressure was answered by the table at once. As soon as my hands came to life, they put me in a world where everything was an exchange of pressures. These pressures gathered together in shapes, and each one of the shapes had meaning. As a child I spent hours leaning against objects and letting them lean against me . . . it is more than seeing them, it is tuning in on them and allowing the current they hold to connect with one's own, like electricity. To put it differently, this means an end of living in front of things and a beginning of living with them. Never mind if the word sounds shocking, for this is love."

Touch as Contact

As Lusseyran so eloquently imparts, touch creates contact. While we are taking in sensory impressions we are likewise sending out impressions of ourselves. One example of this two-way communication can be found in massage. Any good massage practitioner will attest to the phenomenon that giving a good massage is almost as therapeutic as receiving one. Likewise, taking an object in our hands or even brushing against it with the hip establishes a relationship. We are in constant touch with a myriad of substances that lie outside our boundaries of self. Our feet touch the ground, our seats meet the chair, our hands touch hundreds of objects each day from the food we eat to the beds we sleep in at night. But for human beings, the touch of another living creature is special. It gives reassurance, warmth, pleasure, comfort and renewed vigor. It tells us that we are not alone.

We use the term 'being in touch with reality', which implies that our entire sense of what is real is shaped by our sense of touch. In our society, to be deprived of contact with fellow humans is a severe form of punishment (e.g., incarceration and especially solitary confinement). In times of stress our need for human contact is even more intense. During these periods we are especially grateful for reassurance that our troubles are acknowledged and shared. At these times we yearn for the release of tension that physical contact can bring.

Hugs are a very specialized way of touching that help us to contact, connect, and care. Hugs do more for people than simply making us feel good (although helping each other to feel better is a very important function of hugs). An embrace can convey gladness and joy and be a way of sharing those happy feelings with others. Or it can be an overture of affection and sexual attraction. Hugs can also communicate other information, such as sympathy, understanding, and reassurance, over and above everyday verbal and nonverbal messages.

According to my friend, Judith Lerner-Taylor, a former nurse and professional dancer, hugs are a vehicle for transmitting a kinesthetic memory (imprint) of each other's energy. She claims that the energy we share when we hug is like a nonphysical identification, as unique as our own fingerprints.

Perhaps more than any other form of touch, hugs demonstrate the magic that is referred to in the statement, "Well, I guess I haven't lost my touch." Virginia Satir, a popular Californian writer and social scientist, claims that everyone needs four hugs a day for survival, eight for maintenance, and twelve for growth. A similar message can be found in an early Sally Forth cartoon. In the first frame of the cartoon, the young daughter embraces her mother, Sally, when she walks in the door after a long hard day at work. Sally's frown changes to a smile and her beaten posture immediately straightens. The precocious daughter summarizes the events as she tells her step-dad, "A hug a day keeps the psychiatrist away."

Although hugs can be a source of renewal and appreciation, indifferent or halfhearted hugs send a very different message. These kinds of embraces lack the nurturing aspect. To test this theory for yourself, find someone to share a variety of hugs, some which are nurturing and some which are not. In an 'A-frame' hug you and your partner meet at the top, but from the neck down, there is no body contact. The feet are farthest away and you sort of lean heads toward each other like an A-frame house. Another halfhearted embrace is called 'half a chest is better than none'. In this hug, you touch each other with only half your chest. Similarly, 'hip to hip' hugs meet only at the hip. Hip to hip huggers stand side to side, arms around each other's waists, with one person's right side meeting the other's left. 'Burp the baby' refers to the action of patting your partner on the back in the hug. A pat on the back tends to make the other person less sensual, and thereby less threatening. Does it also make the hug less intimate? What do you think? In the 'jock twirl' you pick up your partner and twirl him around, sometimes until he becomes dizzy and begs for mercy. It is more an expression of power than a gesture of affection. Along the same lines, the 'bear hug' is an attempt to squeeze the breath out of your partner. The object is to squeeze as hard as you can and to compete to see who has the strongest hold. In contrast to all of these is the nurturing hug, in which neither partner is overpowered or avoided. In the nurturing hug, two people stand facing each other and body contact is established.

Touch for Healing

Many of the stresses of adult life can be alleviated with the soothing hand of a caring friend. Massage can soothe backs and necks that cramp up after a long day at the office. Stroking can invigorate the exhausted or over-strained muscles that result from heavy physical labor or excessive exercise. Learned hands can ease circulatory problems suffered by people who are disabled or bedridden or people who do not otherwise get enough exercise. For those who do play sports, or for those who wish to play at a peak level, therapeutic massage is an invaluable aid, since relaxation is essential for optimal performance. For active people, healing touch can increase circulation and prevent tightness and injury.

The skin is the largest organ in the body. Our outer sheaths were designed to protect sensitive inner organs from viruses, bacteria, microorganisms, and other toxic agents of infection. The skin also needs to touch and be touched in order to survive. When we are ill or injured in some way, our hands naturally gravitate towards the hurts that need soothing. An instinctive reaction to a tummy ache, for example, is to circle the belly. Without even thinking about it, we rest our hands on fevered brows and rub our foreheads when they ache. A natural response to an aching lower back is to support it with our hands. When we are alone and in pain, we cradle and hug ourselves. We rest tired heads in our hands and unconsciously massage aching limbs.

Not surprisingly, emotional pain evokes a similar instinctive response. Sentient beings cry with heads in their hands. Rocking and hugging our own bodies can be a comfort when we find ourselves in shock or in mourning. In troubled times, a strong shoulder to cry on or an outstretched hand to hold on to is a welcome sight. For many people, one touch from an empathetic soul can be more therapeutic than a thousand well-intended words. Holding and stroking convey comfort and reassurance.

The Instinctive Need for Touch

The loving hands of parents push and pull in ways that are essential for growth. As long as the need to touch and be touched is satisfied, healthy children thrive and even a sick child grows more healthy and strong. When tactile needs are inhibited, development may be impaired. Foundling children who have been stroked and held by nurses tend to grow more and resist illness better than those who have not had tactile encounters. This is also true for premature babies kept in hospital nurseries. Hugs and cuddles we receive as babies and as adults help us to realize that we are accepted and loved. Over forty years ago, S.M. Jourard showed that our perception of how much we are touched by other people seems to be tied to our self-esteem. Experiments with infant primates and observations of human babies and other mammals have confirmed that physical contact with a warm, caring mother is essential and that physical deprivation can stunt physical and emotional growth.

Psychological Touch

Language demonstrates a strong coupling in our minds between physical and emotional touch. For example, have you ever used or heard this expression, "Jack certainly is touchy today"? A mind/body association is also illustrated by the phrase, "Jack is acting a little funny, like he was touched in the head." Words also reflect a positive affiliation between psychological and physical touch. "I am touched by your kindness." When we are affected in a deep emotional way, we say that we are 'touched'.

Whatever our age or stage in life, we all could use a little more human contact. Holding and stroking express a tenderness and caring that show us we are not alone. Without the warmth of a friendly hand to link and soothe us, we are denied one of our most vital avenues for communication: giving and receiving. We recognize the importance of the physical bond in establishing and maintaining psychological contact when we request of a friend who is moving far away to 'Keep in touch'.

Touch as a Communication Tool

Even when our muscles are not particularly stiff, most of us enjoy a mas
sage. Why? For the stimulus, for the contact, for the healing – certainly
these are all benefits of touch. But there is another advantage that ha
not been fully explored. That advantage lies in the fact that touch is on
of the most powerful channels for human communication. It is as true for
adults as it is for tiny babies that communication is a key factor in ou
enjoyment of touch. Try massaging your own arm or neck – it feels good
but not blissful. Likewise, a massage from an indifferent or distracte
therapist is far from a satisfying experience. The delight of a good mas
sage comes largely from the immediate physical knowledge that anothe
person is totally devoting their time and energy to making you feel wonder
ful. Even if the practitioner is getting paid for a service, the intent affect
the service. Although there may be many ways to communicate, toucl
is the one medium that speaks the brain's native language.

One of the great tragedies of our day is that certain segments of th
population suffer a great lack of human touch. Widows and widowers
people in hospitals and nursing homes, and persons with cancer o
Acquired Immune Deficiency Syndrome (AIDS) are some of the group
most in need of physical contact.

There are several prescriptions for the lack of physical contact in you
own life. Some of these remedies include learning to express yourself witl
touch, exchanging loving massages with a spouse, child, or friend, an
giving and receiving lots of hugs. When you become more adept at incor
porating this often neglected physical sense into your daily routine, perhap
you will be motivated to share with those who rarely get to experienc
touch at all. You may want to volunteer some time and a warm embrac
or a loving massage for patients confined to institutions, hospices, o
hospital beds. After all, whenever you touch someone else, you receiv
touch in return.

In much the same way as the Body Work of Chapter 5 provided
forum in which to learn and play with concepts of time and space, s
can the following kinesthetic exercises teach many things about the phys
ical concepts of touching, sensing, stroking, and holding. Enjoy!

Body Work

1. *The Energy of Touch*. For this demonstration, you need a group of people. They may or may not already know each other.

   a) All you do is form a circle, close the eyes, and hold hands. This simple act of joining together in touch can be a very powerful experience. Ask yourself if the physical connection creates an energy manifested by the group? Does it create an extra energy in you?

   b) Release hands and move the circle a little closer. Let your arms encircle the waists of people who are standing on either side of you. Close your eyes again or if everyone agrees, keep your eyes open. Ask yourself if there is a special energy to this group. Did the group hug help to bring more energy out?

2. *Exploring through Touch*. You can do this exploration with a friend, or you can explore your own limbs. Take your friend's hand in your own (or alternately take hold of your own foot) and explore the entire extremity with touch. You can poke, stroke, shake, smooth, support – all with the intention of learning more about this strange appendage you hold in your hand. Examine all the surfaces, crannies, lines and bumps. After about five minutes, stop your activity (and if you are working with a partner, switch roles). What sort of information could you gather through the sense of touch? How did it feel to be explored in this way?

3. *Head and Neck Massage* is a wonderful way to experience the two-way communication of touch. I recommend that you set some time aside (about half an hour would be sufficient) in which to exchange massages with a partner. That way each of you gets to be on both the giving and the receiving end. Both roles have advantages. Although I strongly recommend creativity in your massage technique, this segment will provide a road map to get you started. (Caution: Make sure that you and your partner have no medical history of injury or other health problems with the spine and/or head.)

   Seat the person who is on the receiving end in an upright chair. The person who will be giving the massage stands behind. Massage practitioners, take a deep breath and relax, then place the palms of the hands on your partner's forehead. Make tiny circles around the forehead and spiral those circles down to a place just above the ear, at the temples. Bring the hands back to the forehead, a little lower down. Again spiral circles down to the temple. Continue in this way all the way down the face, under the eyes, around the cheekbones, under the nose and around the lips and chin, always finishing the strokes back around the temples just above the ear. Stroke behind the ears, underneath and on top and gently pull the earlobes to stimulate and refresh the ears. Press down on the shoulders and knead the large masses of tissue around the shoulder area. Now bring the hands along both sides of the spine at the back of the neck. Use your thumbs to make tiny circles all the way up to the back of the head, at the ridge. Now make tiny circles along the occipital ridge out towards the ears. Work through the hair as if you are giving a shampoo. When you have 'shampooed' the entire crown, bring the hands back to the forehead. Let them rest there for a moment, and gently release. You have completed the massage. Now switch places . . . it is your turn to receive.

4. *Knots*. With a group of people, form a circle. First everyone grabs a right hand of someone other than the person next to you. Then everyone grabs a left hand. Try to get everyone back to a circle. (This will only work if you have less than fourteen people.) When the group is all holding hands, tell them the name of the exercise is 'Knots'. Ask others and yourself, does it ever feel like life is one big knot? Now try to untie the physical knot, and tell how that feels.

5. *Raindrops*. Arrange a group of people into two circles (one in back of the other). Have them tap the back of the person in front of them (lightly and fairly fast) with an open palm for a couple of minutes. Next have everyone make 'raindrops' lightly with their fingertips on people's heads. It is important to stress that this exercise is for everyone and that all have a responsibility to give feedback and ask the person giving the massage to reach a certain spot, or to be gentler or firmer, or to stop. Have each individual make a quick scan of their mental state, before and after the 'raindrops'.

6. *Contact Mirroring.* Physical contact can teach us a lot about the effect touch can have on another. This exercise employs contact and pressure as a tool to greater self-awareness. Contact mirroring involves mirroring (see exercises in Chapter 12 on **reaction** and **response**) **plus** an exchange of weight. It involves actual touching, as opposed to simple gesture. If the leader presses in, so does the follower. If the leader leans out, the follower does the same. This way, the leader cannot only see the effects of an action, (s)he can also literally feel it. Choose a partner and without speaking or using body language in any way, mutually decide who will be the first to lead. The leader initiates pressing, pulling, or leaning actions and the follower mirrors the motions. After about five minutes of moving in this way, change roles. What did you observe?

*   *   *   *   *

Not all interactions with others are happy ones. Sometimes our touch is rejected or ignored. We aren't always able to coordinate our needs with those of other people around us. This can create conflict. Perhaps surprisingly, perhaps not, conflict is one situation where much self-learning can occur. How will we react? How will we respond to the threat? The all-important subject of **reaction** vs. **response** is the final Bodylesson.

Chapter 12

REACTION vs. RESPONSE

*You must begin to trust yourself. If you do not then
you will forever be looking to others to prove your own
merit and you will never be satisfied.*
– Jane Roberts in The Nature of Personal Reality

Are Humans Governed by Natural Laws of Action and Reaction?

For the most part, human behavior does seem to be governed by the law of action-reaction. However, humans have the potential of realizing that they can respond, act, and feel any way that they choose. Lack of freedom does not come from other people or outside conditions, but from internal thinking processes. One way to give up freedom is by not allowing yourself a choice. You are not free when you give up the choice of how to respond in a given situation. You are not free when you react.

Response-ability

Re-'acting' implies simply acting again, that no new original response is called forth to meet the challenge. Responding is a higher-level process which involves knowledge of yourself and the situation at hand, and it is based on freedom of choice. Reacting occurs on a baser, more instinctual level and involves no choice whatsoever. For instance, when a friend criticizes you, you may react by feeling hurt or angry. The first step to freedom is realizing that you have other options. In this case, perhaps you could think, "Jan is only criticizing me because she is very critical of herself," or, "Jan is having a bad day and she is just expressing that by criticizing me." You can choose to respond without taking your friend's actions personally. In most situations that require a response, you can choose among many different responses. Do you want to succumb to a reaction that makes you feel bad about yourself, or do you want to choose a response that makes you feel good? The ideas and exercises in this chapter are designed to help you realize that you can choose how you want to respond and act and be. This 'ability to respond' to any situation is at the root (literally and figuratively) of true 'responsibility'.

It never occurs to most people to examine their own responsibility in what comes up in their lives. If something 'good' happens, it was luck. If something 'bad' occurs, it was someone or something else's fault. Most of us see ourselves as victims of circumstances. This passive attitude creates a sense of powerlessness. On the other hand, if we see ourselves as the primary cause of what happens to us, we gain personal power. We then have an ability to exercise control over our situations. This ability is 'responsibility', or the ability to respond.

Choosing is an act of responsibility that gets us out of the attitude of the victim ("I have to") and in touch with our own free will ("I want to"). Times when we feel 'stuck' may be the times when we most need to take responsibility for our situation by accepting that right now we are stuck. That doesn't mean we will always be stuck or that we are "giving in". It is simply affirming where we are right now. This act may not alter the situation, but it allows us to approach the challenge from a healthier perspective and a fresh point of view.

Most people 'respond' in habitual ways (i.e., they react), rather than examining potential responses before they act. Many men and women react impulsively and without thought. Other people react to you in whatever way they have been programmed. True power comes with the knowledge that you have a choice. Your response does not need to change the other person. In fact, it is just about impossible to change someone else no matter how hard you try.

You cannot and do not need to change anyone else'. Trying to change someone else creates low self-esteem, poor communications, trying to control others, denying your true feelings, repression of anger, and perfectionism & overachievement tendencies. It makes you into an ardent approval seeker, trying to win acceptance from everyone to compensate for lack of self-acceptance. Approximately 96% of Americans exhibit traits such as these.

Even though you cannot change how others act, you can change how you respond to others' actions. You can choose not to re-'act' the same annoying patterns that your companions have displayed. You can choose to feel good. You can realize that you are not dependent on other people acting in certain ways to make you feel good. Before you can attract people who will support, appreciate, and understand you, you first must choose to support, appreciate, and understand yourself.

Dealing with Conflict

One of the more uncomfortable situations that requires human response (rather than reaction) is conflict. Most of us either avoid it or pretend conflict doesn't exist. We fear conflict because we have been conditioned to believe that it is wrong to argue, fight, or disagree. There are many unpleasant feelings that go along with conflict, such as hurt, anger, frustration, resentment, and disappointment. However, conflict is a natural phenomenon among creatures. What a boring world it would be if everyone agreed on every issue! The trick is not to deny our differences or to run from them, but to deal with them straight on. If you find the courage to respond to conflict, you will reduce stress and your relationships will improve. This does not mean that you will always be ecstatic about the outcome. It does mean that you can stop hiding your true feelings and avoiding situations that might require you to reveal those feelings.

People typically deal with conflict in one of three fashions: non-assertively, assertively, or aggressively. (These three behavior styles actually fall along a continuum and any response to a situation probably contains elements of all three.) Non-assertiveness means being totally concerned with the rights of others at the expense of your own rights. The problem with non-assertiveness is that it leaves you with a lot of unsatisfied needs. Aggressiveness is the opposite, getting what you want, 'come hell or high water', no matter whom it hurts. The flaw in sheer aggression is that it leads to poor interpersonal relationships and unsatisfied intimacy needs. Assertiveness is a skill of moderation. It requires finding a balance between satisfying your needs and maintaining good relationships with others.

Behaving assertively is more difficult for some than for others, but there are a number of techniques that can help everyone. These include using assertive body language, the 'broken record' approach, escalation, delaying, clearly asking for what you want, and deciding to compromise or deciding not to assert your desires in a given situation.

The *broken record approach* is exactly what it sounds like. You continue to repeat your message until it finally makes an impression. When you start at an appropriate response, but realize the option to get more aggressive in order to get a message across you are making use of *escalation*. *Delaying* means postponing a discussion until some given time in the future. If you are completely stumped about what to do in a situation, delaying can buy you some time to think about your options. One caution is not to postpone indefinitely. Instead of leaving a discussion with an open-ended stall, "I don't want to talk now", make a definite date to talk in the future, "I'd rather not discuss this while driving, let's make time to talk after dinner tomorrow night." Assertive communication involves two basic skills. One is to make sure you understand the other person (by asking for *clarification* of his/her *expectations*). The second skill is *stating clearly what you want*.

Saying what you mean effectively and clearly can be enhanced by using the DESC model. DESC stands for Describe, Express, Specify and Consequence. Describe a verbal picture of the situation. Express what you feel about the situation. Specify several ways that you would like the other person's behavior to change. Consequence refers to specifying what you will do if the other person's behavior changes to your satisfaction **and** saying what you will do if the situation doesn't change. This model helps you to plan what you are going to say ahead of time and to practice before you get into the conflict situation. To review, the formula goes, ("When ____ happens, I feel ____. I would prefer that you do ____. If you do ____, I will ____ and if you don't I will ____"). You fill in the blanks.

Assertiveness also allows you the freedom to *compromise* or even *to decide not to assert* your views right now if either option can further your interests. Remember that certain techniques may not be appropriate for a given situation. Use the tools that help and dismiss options that do not.

Body Language

The way you respond is not only a function of what you say but also *how* you say it. Let's say your supervisor asks you how your work is going. What kind of message do you send when your eyes look away and down towards the floor? What would you think of a coworker who was constantly swaying and shifting weight whenever (s)he carried on a conversation? What if (s)he spoke in a voice that was always hesitant and whiny?

Body language is made up of all the silent, subtle, and often subconscious little movements that tell us so much about what we are really thinking. Some gestures are not so subtle and are easily interpreted. Everyone in our culture recognizes the messages behind shaking hands, a mouth wide open in surprise, a thumbs-down signal, or applause at the end of a show.

In some ways, body language is clearer than our spoken language because we do not always have complete control of our physical responses. A bodily reaction happens suddenly, spontaneously, and in answer to something that has been said or done. Involuntary movements cannot be disguised nearly as well as words. Blushing, for example, is an uncontrolled body signal. If you were embarrassed about something that just occurred, you would blush immediately, not several hours later.

Some signals are not so obvious. Recognizing body signs is one thing, interpreting them is quite another. (See Chapter 8 on Expression for more information on body language.) Does the man who is stroking his head indicate someone who is lost in thought? Or does it mean he has a headache? Is the woman rubbing her hands expecting something, or are her hands merely cold? Many messages depend on the person who is sending them and/or the environment in which they take place. Beware of assuming that you know what the other fellow means when he fidgets with a tie or pats his hair during an argument. Misread signals can add to misunderstandings and bad feelings. They can accentuate rather than mitigate confusion. However, you can effectively use body language to accent your own responses with clear assertive signals. Clear messages will go a long way towards alleviating and avoiding conflict.

Consider the handshake. Shaking hands is an age-old gesture that says, "I come bearing no arms. I come in peace." An assertive handshake is offered with a strong, friendly, open hand. This can be contrasted with the aggressive hand, which traps you in a vice-like grip that will not let go. The assertive hand is also very different from the non-assertive, submissive, even weak hand that is extended limply. Just as a handshake can affirm a verbal response, so can other bodily gestures attest to the veracity of our words. What do your movements say about your ability to respond?

Physical Response

We can learn a lot about reaction and response by paying attention to the way we physically respond to a situation. Our physical bodies can tactilely and tangibly sense the effect of another person's actions. When we are pushed, we know how it feels. Our bodies can kinetically feel the effects of their own actions on another human being. If I am arm wrestling, and I make a quick flick of the wrist, I will kinesthetically perceive one of two alternative responses. Either I will feel my partner's hand going down in capitulation or I will feel increased resistance coming to meet my force.

Careful observation of another figure in motion can point out differences (and similarities) between the ways that I and other humans respond physically. Mimicking those movements exactly will show how it feels to move in that new way. Pitting ourselves physically against someone else can bring to light powers that everyone possesses but few people realize they have.

Martial Arts – New Paradigms for Kinetic Response

Tai Chi Chuan (or simply Tai Chi) teaches softness in the face of hardness. The skills it teaches are absorbing, neutralizing, and redirecting force. Aikido teaches blending with another's energy rather than resisting. These two alternative methods for dealing with conflict can add to your repertoire of responses. The more options from which you have to choose, the less likely you will be to simply react out of habit. Because they allow people to pit their physical responses against those of another human being in an atmosphere of learning and fun, these two martial arts can bring out hidden powers in participants. Through diligent practice of Aikido or Tai Chi Chuan, many people notice a marked change in their daily life. Devotees report that decisions become easier to make, responses are quicker and more facile, and that they have become more peaceful and relaxed inside. In short, many find that they have gained a greater control over the emotions, body, and mind.

Mirroring is another method that can demonstrate many valuable lessons about action and reaction. It is an improvisational technique that requires two participants who have an active stake in making the exercise a success. The initiating partner must ensure that the movements are regular and slow enough so that they can be duplicated. The responding partner's task is to follow along without delay. Ideally, two equivalent but opposite motions (as in a mirror) will be going on at the same time, neither one jumping before nor lagging behind the other. Simultaneity is maintained as new motions begin, change, and follow through. Successful mirroring improves nonverbal communication and receptivity to what will happen next.

Skillful mirroring translates into several types of reward with regard to reaction and response. First, imitating develops an ability to perceive and reproduce movement. Second, remaining synchronized with a partner teaches how to respond without delay. Third, concentrating on the action to be mirrored exercises the ability to direct and sustain a focus. Fourth, since every detail must be reproduced, the follower gets a kinesthetic sense of what it is like to move like someone else, to be like someone else, to voluntarily experience the different kinds of motion that are natural to other human beings. An experiential discovery of new movement possibilities comes out of mirroring. Many benefits derive from the act of truly watching and responding to another person.

Body Work

1. *Body Language.* This exercise demonstrates in a graphic way that the way you respond to someone else is not only a function of what you say but *how* you say it.

   a) Say the words "Hello, how are you today?" as you mimic these actions (eyes down, swaying and shifting weight, weak hesitant voice), and notice how you feel.

   b) Now, lean forward with glaring eyes and a pointing finger (an aside: remember that whenever you point a finger at someone else, four fingers are pointing back at you). Make your voice very strong, so loud that others might say you are shouting. You might also try out some alternate arm and hand positions. Clench both hands into very tight fists and hold them at your sides. Or try putting your hands on your hips or crossing your arms. Hold the poses for one minute each and note how you feel. In each position shout, "Hello, how are you today?" Repeat the phrase one last time with teeth clenched so hard that no words come out at all, or if the words do emerge, it is only in short fitful bursts. How do you feel now?

   c) Now assume a comfortable erect posture directly facing the person to whom you are speaking. Relax your shoulders and maintain good eye contact. In a clear, steady voice say, "Hello, how are you today?" Again pay attention to how you feel and put this feeling into words. Either write it down or tell somebody else, so that you can better remember your experiences.

Do any of the body positions complement aggressive behavior? Which, if any, correspond with assertiveness? Which goes along with non-assertiveness?

2. *Mirroring*
   a) In a typical introductory mirroring exercise, partners begin by facing each other. One partner takes the initiator role for a given amount of time, say five minutes, and then roles are switched. This allows both partners to take responsibility for leading. It also allows both partners (when each assumes the follower role) to sense their bodies moving in a way that is probably very foreign to them.
   b) In a more advanced form of mirroring, the leader and follower roles can be performed by teams. Teams face each other, and one entire team first takes the initiator role. In this case, each person must not only mirror a counterpart, but must maintain the same relationship (proximity) to his/her own team members as the counterpart on the other team.

3. *Responding to Physical Conflict.* 'Push Hands' is a traditional Tai Chi exercise, in which two partners alternately use force and yielding to a force as a means of testing their ability to respond. The object is to upset the balance of the other while maintaining one's own stability.
   a) First, establish a baseline for comparison to the push hands approach. Ask a partner to come towards you, straight on, as if in an attack. Try to fend off the action by standing as firm and strong as you can. If you are pushed with a strong force, meet that force with an opposing push of your own. What happens?
   b) Now, meet the attack with a different plan of action. This time, your aim is to consciously respond in a way that will soften or neutralize the threat. As your friend draws closer, allow your body to give. Give way to any pressure that your opponent may exert, no matter how slight. If a feather were placed on your arm, the

arm would slowly sink under its weight, you are so receptive to the force. When you respond in this way, what happens to conflict? Is non-resistance a more successful defense? When you respond in this way, you are in control, and you can usually watch your partner follow through until (s)he falls to the floor.

c) Once you begin to acquire the skill of being in constant synch, the next step is to close your eyes and practice the same techniques. This action greatly enhances sensitivity. You begin to understand what is going on inside your opponent's body, and this will increase your understanding of what is going on inside your own body. The partner becomes a mirror in which you see your own reflection.

As with mirroring, the chief value of push hands training is the heightened sensitivity that you develop by being in constant touch with a partner. With practice, you will be able to tell if your partner is tense, which of their feet carries the most weight, which part of the foot is experiencing the greatest pressure, the degree of pressure and even the direction in which it is being applied.

4. *Verbal Response.* The philosophy of responding rather than reacting can also be applied to verbal battles. In order to really respond, you must concentrate on what your partner is saying and make room in your head for the message. In a technique called 'verbal mirroring', you reflect back your partner's message until (s)he indicates it is accurate, then you respond specifically to what you have heard (resisting the temptation to introduce another topic or to express your opinion). If, after you have verbally mirrored your partner, you disagree or want to present your own view, then it is your turn to be 'mirrored'. It is your partner's job to reflect back your message until you feel heard. Verbal mirroring allows you to make deep emotional contact and to really understand where another human being is coming from. It is another option for dealing with conflict, rather than always trying to win an argument or prove a point.

Think of a conflict in your life in which verbal mirroring might be appropriate. (Hint: Such techniques are usually more effective with a partner who agrees to use the method with you. In cases when you or the other party is not open to considering another point of view, e.g., your 12-year-old daughter wants to date a man aged 31, this method is definitely not appropriate.) Plan how you will make use of verbal mirroring. Then do it. What happens when you use the method?

*   *   *   *   *

Chapter 13

DISCIPLINES

Without discipline, there is no life.
– Katharine Hepburn

As has been said many times throughout the book, the concepts underlying the Bodylessons are not new; they derive from tried and true methods
established over ages and ages of experiences. Also it is no secret that
many of the Body Work exercises at the end of each chapter have been
influenced by organized disciplines. Disciplines impose a systematic method,
a state of order upon investigations into the natural physical world. To
create this work, I have borrowed freely from many teachings and have
tried to extrapolate useful techniques from each teaching, training, or
branch of knowledge.

The term 'discipline' may erroneously conjure up a one-sided sense of
strictness, firmness, or an unyielding quality. Let us remember that the
term also derives 'from the disciples' or 'from those close to the source
of inspiration and light'.

Some Guidelines

For those readers whose interest might be sparked by any of the disciplines that have been mentioned in *Bodylessons*, a capsule summary of
each of those teachings has been included here. Many of you may wish
to obtain more information or may be inspired to further pursue some
particular brand of physical training. To aid in that quest, addresses for
each organization's headquarters are printed when available, below the

capsule summaries. For each discipline covered in this chapter, particularly applicable Bodylessons are noted in parentheses just to the right of the summary heading. This way, readers who wish to explore organized teachings that enhance selected Bodylessons have some guidance. Although only one Bodylesson is noted in parentheses for each discipline reviewed in this chapter, you may well discover that, for you, a number of Bodylessons may be enhanced by a certain discipline. Also, you may wish to utilize a variety of techniques to accentuate your favorite Bodylesson. By all means, feel free to follow your instincts.

However, please be discriminating in your studies of any of the disciplines outlined in this chapter or any disciplines you happen to find on your own. I hope that your work with *Bodylessons* has helped you to see that the only real truth that you can know is the truth you experience for yourself. A process that holds great meaning and guidance for me may not be rigorous enough to capture your interest. Or a physical discipline that may be thoroughly enjoyable for a friend may seem silly to you. Or vice versa. See for yourself. Be open to trying lots of options, but listen to your own inner voice and body to measure how much value a particular teaching has for you. Remember, the best expert is **you**.

A final note: this list of body-based techniques is by no means all-inclusive. I have attempted to provide introductory information about the disciplines that have been most influential in my life and in the creation of this book. Many other excellent methods exist, but where I have no firsthand experience, I leave the path uncensored and uncriticized for you to explore.

*   *   *   *   *

Gurdjieff Movements (AWARENESS)

The 'movements' are one of the techniques handed down by students of the Gurdjieff tradition. Gurdjieff movements are designed to spark an awareness of something higher and an emotional response to complex motor demands. Movements are precisely defined positions of the hands, arms, feet, legs and head, sometimes with voice participation. They are performed in changing formations to specially-composed music. The music sounds very much like Persian Sufi melodies. Often, the movements are so complex that one cannot perform them when thinking about what (s)he is doing. Practitioners of Gurdjieff movements bring an inordinate amount of attention to the task of remembering and executing the difficult maneuvers. Even with such concentration and effort, the movements could not be replicated without relying on 'something higher' to coordinate the movement of self with others in changing formations. Gurdjieff practitioners are not very forthcoming about sharing their practices with outsiders. None of the movements are described for public use in any text, but you can witness them in the Peter Brook film, *Meetings With Remarkable Men.*

Gurdjieff Foundation
123 E. 63rd Street
New, York, NY 10021
www.gurdjieff_foundation_newyork.org

Feldenkrais (FOCUSING)
Feldenkrais work allows the body to reeducate the brain through seemingly simple movements. Moshe Feldenkrais, an Israeli physicist and sixth dan black belt in judo, devised the method in the 1940's to heal his own knees. By changing his body's relationship to gravity, his knees became fully functional.

Lessons are dispensed in two forms: private table work sessions (Functional Integration) and group movement classes (Awareness Through Movement). Both train you to use your muscles to teach the motor cortex that there are freer and more relaxed ways to walk, sit, carry, stand, and lie.

Awareness Through Movement classes typically last about an hour. Most of the movements are done while lying or sitting on the floor in order to minimize the impact of gravity. The movements are simple, repetitive, and undemanding. Tiny movements repeated again and again allow you to find the most efficient way of making the motion and to ingrain that pattern into your brain. Over a thousand minute movement sequences help people reeducate their skeletal, muscular, and nervous systems. Feldenkrais theory is to teach the body to expand to its full range of motion in order to help the self reach its full potential.

Feldenkrais Guild
3611 SW Hood Ave., Suite 100
Portland, OR 97239
800–775–2118
www.feldenkraisquild.com

Alexander Technique (POSTURE)
The Alexander Technique teaches you to replace unhealthy movement patterns with ones that you have consciously chosen. The emphasis is on lengthening the body through proper positioning (usually up and out with a slight cervical nod) of your head and neck. F.M. Alexander was a 19th century actor who suffered from a series of episodes during which he lost his voice. In an effort to find out why, he rigged up mirrors to observe himself from many angles as he stood and spoke. Alexander discovered a tendency to pull his head backward and down, affecting his whole body alignment and creating an inability to speak.

Alexander therapists believe that the dynamic relationship between our heads and bodies is the primary mechanism that controls human coordination. One can discover the influence of the head on the rest of the spine by becoming aware of the area and experimenting with different head positions. The method is applied to activities such as walking, standing up from a chair, playing a musical instrument, or speaking. Teachers verbally guide a student's thinking about how to execute an action and use faint touch (less than a smidgen of pressure) to influence change. A new way of performing emerges. Singers and musicians produce more pleasing and resonant sounds. Moving becomes more graceful and elegant. The Alexander Technique can prevent fatigue caused by excess tension and is recommended by health professionals for preventive care of the neck, back and spine.

For more information on The Alexander Technique:
The Alexander Foundation
The Barstow/Alexander Institute
Doane College
1014 Boswell Ave.
Crete, NE. 68333–2430

Trager Psychophysical Integration (PLAY)

Trager workers believe that pleasurable stimulation is the most effective teacher for the body. They use gentle, rhythmic, non-intrusive movement to generate pleasurable sensory signals. Feelings of movement without effort are thought to release tensions brought on by trauma, illness, or emotional wounds. Milton Trager, MD, discovered the work when he was an eighteen-year-old professional boxer in Miami. One day he traded rubdowns with his trainer, got a strong positive response, and went home and worked on his father's sciatica. After two sessions the pain never returned. Trager work has two components: table work and movement reeducation (Mentastics). Trager table work consists of gentle stretching and rhythmic rocking and shaking motions guided by the client's own natural body responses. Mentastics are light, simple ways of moving the body to create awareness, improve function, and recall the feeling of lightness and freedom. The name, Mentastics, intentionally blends the word 'mental' with 'gymnastics'. The movements simulate a kind of constantly fluttering wave motion.

The Trager Institute
21 Locust Avenue
Mill Valley, CA 94941
415–388–2688
www.trager.com

Hatha Yoga (RELATIONSHIP)

Yoga literally means to join together or to yoke. We can think of this joining as the union of the self with something higher, like a God, or as the union of the body with the mind, or as the union of the self with other selves. Raja yoga, the royal path (also called ashtanga yoga or the eight-fold path) includes the teachings of all paths of yoga. Asanas are specific body positions that help stretch the body and calm the mind. Asanas are perfected by relaxing, not forcing the effort. Breath control is coordinated with the postures. As you breathe in, your body expands and as you breathe out it contracts. Asanas are best performed slowly, steadily, and with attention on letting go of unnecessary tensions and easy, deep breathing. After a series of three or four poses, students relax in one of the resting poses. Hatha Yoga trains the body in relaxation and control while it trains the mind in awareness.

American Yoga Association
P.O. Box 19986
Sarasota, FL. 34276
941–927–4977
www.americanyogaassociation.org

Psychocalisthenics (ENERGY)
Psychocalisthenics are a set routine of twenty-three exercises that were strictly developed to energize and revitalize the body. The exercises are based on elemental calisthenic movements in combination with yoga asanas. Psychocalisthenics are performed more swiftly than hatha yoga doctrine would dictate and the accompanying breathing is designed to bring maximum airflow into each area of the body sequentially. Inhalations are always taken through the nose and the exhalations leave through the mouth. The breath is the 'inspiration' for the movements.

Oscar Ichazo, who created the system in 1958, claims that psychocalisthenics awakens the organism in a serial fashion, and produces a flash of vital energy through all the organs, glands and tissue. The exercises focus on five centers: the cranial cavity (the intellectual center), the thoracic cavity (the feeling center), the abdominal cavity (the sense of plenitude), the pelvic cavity (vitality), and the dorsal cavity (the structural and coordinating center). Individuals feel more energetic after completing the series and a feeling of happiness often emerges at the end of a set. Ichazo intended these sensations to be used as an aid to meditation.

Arica Institute, Inc.
UK 10 Landmark Lane
PO Box 645
Kent CT 06757–1526
+1 860 927 1006
taichi.gn.apc.org/arica.htm

Aikido (REACTION)

Aikido is a Japanese art of self-defense that evolved in the last few decades. It emerged directly out of the mystical experience and mastery of martial arts attained by Morehei Uyeshiba. The word Aikido is literally translated as the way (Do) of harmony (Ai) with the spirit of the universe (Ki). With Aikido the spirit is of 'blending' with a partner, not of fighting an opponent. There is practice attacking your partner and defending against attacks. Equally essential is the lack of contests, tournaments, or feeling of competition.

International Aikido Federation
c/o Aikikai Foundation
17–18 Watamatsu-cho
Shinjuku-ku, Tokyo 162
JAPAN
www.aikido_international.org
www.aikido.com

Tai Chi (WEIGHT)

Tai Chi is a martial arts technique that may be more accurately described as a moving meditation. The practice involves internal exercises that circulate, augment and balance the flow of energy in the body. Tai Chi is performed in a set sequence. One foot is always in contact with the floor and the legs act like moveable anchors. The weight must constantly shift and adapt to make smooth transitions. There are many different Tai Chi forms; styles can range from slow and continuous movements to lightning fast defensive acts.

Tai Chi Association
4651 Roswell Road
Atlanta, GA 30342
404–289–5652

Massage (TOUCH)

Massage refers to the physical manipulation of muscles, ligaments, and connective tissue. It has origins in Chinese folk medicine and in the athletic and medical practices of ancient Greece and Rome. Massage can reduce stress, relieve fatigue, soothe aches and pains, facilitate relaxation, and promote a sense of well-being. Physiologically, it increases circulation and releases endorphins, the body's natural painkillers. On an emotional level, massage creates a human bond through touch.

Swedish massage
Swedish massage was developed in the late 1800's. It involves systematic manipulation of skin and muscles through specific rhythmic moves. It can include kneading, tapping, compression, vibration, friction, and flowing strokes.

For more information on Swedish massage:
American Massage Therapy Association
500 Davis Street, Suite 900
Evanston, IL. 60201–4695
1–877–905–2700
www.amtamassage.org

Acupressure and *Shiatsu*
These techniques rely on manual stimulation of pressure points to bring the body's energy into equilibrium.

For more information on Acupressure:
Acupressure Institute
1533 Shattuck Ave.
Berkeley, CA 94709
415–845–1059

For more information on Shiatsu:
Ohashi Institute
147 West 25th St., 8th Floor
New York, NY 10001
800–810–4190
www.ohashi.com

Polarity Therapy
Polarity work, devised by Randolph Stone, attempts to encourage free energy flow in the body through balancing positive and negative energy currents.

For more information on Polarity Therapy
American Polarity Therapy Association
PO Box 19858
Boulder, CO. 80308
303–545–2080
www.polaritytherapy.org

Rolfing and *Hellerwork*
These two therapies use deep tissue massage and direct manipulation to realign the skeleton. Rolfing or 'Structural Integration', devised by Dr. Ida Rolf, focuses more on the body. By the last of ten sessions, the body is longer, the posture straighter, and movement is easier. Rolfing can be painful. Practitioners explain the pain as an offshoot of change that is taking place in the client's body. Hellerwork emphasizes the psychological dimensions of posture and tension.

For more information on Rolfing:
The Rolf Institute ® of Structural Integration
5055 Chaparral Ct., Suite 103
Boulder, CO 8030
800–530–8875
www.rolf.org/institute/index.html

For information on Hellerwork:
The Body of Knowledge
415 Mt. Shasta Blvd. #4
Mt. Shasta, CA 96067
916–926–2500

Dance and Dance Therapy (EXPRESSION)

Movement and dance have long been considered therapeutic for humans of all ages and situations. We dance in times of happiness (weddings) and in times of sadness (mourning).

Dance therapy's influences can be traced back to the modern dance of Isadora Duncan. She focused on the spontaneous and emotional responses that dance can evoke. Although dance therapists grudgingly acknowledge the contributions of ballroom, folk and square dance, the primary influence is from modern dance.

During and after WWII, with the large number of men who needed rehabilitation for emotional disorders, group and activity therapies were explored to handle the increased demand for psychological interventions. In 1942, Marian Chace began dance therapy with psychotic patients at St. Elizabeth's Hospital in Washington, D.C. Dance therapy emphasizes the expression of emotion rather than performance or skills. It encourages 'authentic movement', which is not learned or stylized like ballet, but instead is an expression of one's own movement style. Authentic movement is a spontaneous improvisation of how one feels in the moment, unchecked by the conscious mind. After the movements, dancers talk about what took place and how it felt.

American Dance Therapy Association
2000 Century Plaza, Suite 108
10632 Little Patuxent Parkway
Columbia, MD 21044
410–997–4040
www.adta.org

Reichian Therapies (FLEXIBILITY)

Reichian therapy is the model for a number of body-oriented forms of psychotherapy. It was developed in the 1930's by Dr. Wilhelm Reich, a controversial theoretician who studied under Sigmund Freud. Reich discovered a relationship between tension in the body and rigidity, or psychological limitations in the mind. Reich believed that emotions are a form of energy. Sometimes we tense our muscles to stem the flow of feeling when our emotions become too overwhelming. A one-time muscular defense can lead to chronic tension when we continue to suppress the emotion behind it. Segments of the body that are prone to this kind of tension are around the mouth and eyes, neck, thorax, diaphragm, abdomen and pelvic areas. Reichian therapy gradually softens and removes tension from the top down, through physical manipulation and psychoanalysis.

Bioenergetics
Bioenergetics, founded by Alexander Lowen, is one variation on Reichian psychotherapy. It aims to loosen rigidity from the pelvis up and to help clients integrate their feelings with body awareness. Private sessions combine bodywork with Freudian analysis. Group sessions typically begin with strenuous yoga-like poses and may end with clients throwing temper tantrums to bring about physical and emotional release.

International Institute for Bioenergetic Analysis
144 East 36th St.
New York City, NY 10016
212–532–7742

Radix
Charles Kelly, an experimental psychologist, created Radix in the 1960's. Radix is an offshoot of Reichian therapy that places emphasis on group work over private sessions. Radix is particularly known for helping correct visual disorders. It focuses on improving visual awareness and eye contact as precursors to a more general sense of well-being.

Radix Institute
Route 2, Box 89A
Granbury, TX 76048
817–326–5670

BIBLIOGRAPHY

American Heritage Dictionary. Boston, Massachusetts: Houghton-Mifflin, 1988.

Anderson, Bob. *Stretching.* Bolinas, California: Shelter Publications, Inc., 1980.

Assagoli, R. *Psychosynthesis.* New York, New York: Hobbs, Dorman & Co., 1965.

Ax, Albert F. "The Physiological Differentiation between Fear and Anger in Humans." *Psychosomatic Medicine,* (Volume XV, No. 5, 1953): 434–442.

Bates, W. *Better Eyesight Without Glasses.* New York, New York: Henry Holt & Co., Inc., 1918.

Beattie, Melody. *Codependent No More.* New York, New York: Harper/Hazelden, 1987.

Beck, A.T. "Cognitive Therapy: Nature and Relationship to Behavior Therapy." *Behavior Therapy,* (Volume 1, 1970): 194–200.

Benson, Herbert. *The Relaxation Response.* New York, New York: Avon Books, 1975.

Bloom, Allan. *The Republic of Plato.* New York, New York: Basic Books, Inc., 1968.

Bowlby, John. "Separation Anxiety." *The International Journal of Psycho-analysis,* (Volume XLI, Parts II–III, (1960): 89–113.

Carson, Richard D. *Taming Your Gremlin.* New York, New York: Harper and Row Publishers, 1983.

Center for Positive Living. *Positive Living and Health.* Emmaus, Pennsylvania: Rodale Press, 1990.

Christensen, Alice. *The American Yoga Association Beginner's Manual.* New York, New York: Simon and Schuster, Inc. (A Fireside Book), 1987.

Corbin, Charles & Ruth Lindsey. *Concepts of Physical Fitness with Laboratories,* Dubuque, Iowa: Wm.C. Brown Publishers, 6th edition, 1988.

Cousins, Norman. *Anatomy of an Illness as Perceived by the Patient.* New York, New York: W.W. Norton & Co., Inc., 1979.

Dass, Ram. *Journey of Awakening: A Meditator's Guidebook.* New York, New York: Bantam Books, 1978.

Dixon, Marian. "The Efficacy of Art and Dance Therapy as Thanatological Tools." Unpublished Research. College Park, Maryland: University of Maryland, 1985.

Downing, George. *The Massage Book.* New York, New York: Random House, 1972.

Dychtwald, Ken. *Bodymind.* Los Angeles, California: Jeremy P. Tarcher, Inc., 1986.

Ellis, Alber. *Reason and Emotion in Psychotherapy.* New York, New York: Lyle-Stuart, 1962.

Feldenkrais, Moshe. *The Potent Self.* New York, New York: Harper & Row, Publishers, Inc., 1985.

Feldenkrais, Moshe. *Awareness Through Movement.* New York, New York: Harper & Row, Publishers, Inc., 1977.

Frank, J. *Persuasion and Healing.* Baltimore, Maryland: The Johns Hopkins University Press, 1973.

Gardner, Howard. *Frames of Mind: The Theory of Multiple Intelligences.* New York, New York: Basic Books, 1983.

Gawain, Skakti. *Creative Visualization*. Bantam Books: New York, New York, 1982.

Gerard, R. "Symbolic Visualization – A Method of Psychosynthesis." *Topical Problems in Psychotherapy*. (Vol. 4, 1963): 70–80.

Greenberg, Jerrold S. *Comprehensive Stress Management*. Dubuque, Iowa: Wm.C. Brown Publishers, second edition, 1987.

Groger, Molly. *Eating Awareness Training*. New York, New York: Simon and Schuster, Inc. (Summit Books), 1983.

Hay, Louise. *You Can Heal Your Life*. Santa Monica, California: Hay House, 1987.

Ichazo, Oscar. *Master Level Exercise – Psychocalisthenics*. New York, New York: Sequoia Press, 1986.

Jacobsen, E. *Progressive Relaxation*. Chicago, Illinois: University of Chicago Press, 1942.

James, William. "The Physical Basis of Emotion." *Psychological Review*, (Volume 1, 1894): 516–529.

Leuner, H. "Guided Affective Imagery (GAI)." *American Journal of Psychotherapy*, (1969): 6, 23.

Lusseyran, Jacques. "Sense and Presence." *And There Was Light*, New York, New York: *Parabola Books*, (Vol. XI: 2, 1987).

Luthe, Wolfgang. *Autogenic Therapy*. New York, New York: Grune & Stratton, Vol. I, 1969.

Miller, Neal E. "Learning of Visceral and Glandular Responses." *Science*. (Volume 163, 1969): 434–445.

Millman, Dan. *The Warrior Athlete*. Walpole, New Hampshire: Stillpoint Publishing, 1979.

Morgenroth, Joyce. *Dance Improvisation*. Pittsburgh, Pennsylvania: University of Pittsburgh Press, 1987.

Moss, G.E. *Illness, Immunity and Social Interaction*. New York, New York: John Wiley & Sons, 1973.

Newton, Isaac, 1686. Translated by F. Cajori, *Principia*. Berkeley, California: University of California Press, 1934.

Nicoll, Maurice. *The Mark*. Boston, Massachusetts: Shambala Publications, Inc., 1985.

Perls, F.S. *Gestalt Therapy Verbatim*. New York, New York: Bantam Books, 1974.

Renberger, Boyce and Michael Specter. *Washington Post – Science Notebook*, Monday January 23, 1989: A10.

Richardson, A. *Mental Imagery*. New York, New York: Springer Publishing Company, 1969.

Rolf, Ida P. *Rolfing*. Rochester, Vermont: Healing Arts Press, 1989.

Roman, Sanaya. *Living With Joy*. Tiburon, California: H.J. Kramer, Publishers, 1986.

Roman, Sanaya. *Personal Power through Awareness*. Tiburon, California: H.J. Kramer, Publishers, 1986.

Rossbach, Sarah. *Interior Design with Feng Shui*. Brookline Village, Massachusetts: East West Books, 1990.

Samskrti and Veda. *Hatha Yoga Manual I*, 2nd edition. Honesdale, Pennsylvania: The Himalayan Institute, 1985.

Samskrti and Judith Franks. *Hatha Yoga Manual II* Honesdale, Pennsylvania: The Himalayan Institute, 1982.

Samuels, M. & N. Samuels. *Seeing with the Mind's Eye*. New York, New York: Random House, Inc., 1984.

Satchidananda, Yogiraj Sri Swami. *Integral Yoga Hatha*. New York, New York: Holt, Rinehart and Winston, 1970.

Scholl, Lisette. *Visionetics*. Garden City, New York: Doubleday & Company, Inc., 1978.

Seaward, Brian Luke. *Best Friends: The Psychology of Stress*. Burlington, Vermont: White Pines Publications, 1985.

Simonton, O.C. & S. Matthews-Simonton. "Belief systems and management of the emotional aspects of malignancy." *Journal of Transpersonal Psychology*, 7 (1), (1975): 29–47.

Sinetar, Marsha. *Ordinary People as Monks and Mystics*. Mahwah, New Jersey: Paulist Press, 1986.

Soo, Chee. *The Chinese Art of Tai Chi Chuan*. Northhamptonshire, England: The Aquarian Press (Thorsons Publishing Group), 1984.

Tart, Charles T. *Open Mind, Discriminating Mind*. New York, New York: Harper & Row, Publishers, Inc., 1989.

Transvision Inc. *Body Language – The Silent Communication* (video). Ft. Collins, Colorado: Transvision, Inc., 1987.

Vander, A.J., J.H. Sherman, & D.S Luciano. *Human Physiology: The Mechanisms of Body Function*. New York, New York: McGraw-Hill, Inc., 1980.

Walton, Sally. *Awakening the Inner Dancer*. Minneapolis, Minnesota: Burgess Publishing Company (Alpha Editions), 1986.

Wolpe, Joseph. *The Practice of Behavior Therapy*. New York, New York: Pergamon Press, 1969.

*   *   *   *   *